The Future of the Factory

The Future of the Factory

How Megatrends are Changing Industrialization

Jostein Hauge

OXFORD
UNIVERSITY PRESS

Great Clarendon Street, Oxford, OX2 6DP,
United Kingdom

Oxford University Press is a department of the University of Oxford.
It furthers the University's objective of excellence in research, scholarship,
and education by publishing worldwide. Oxford is a registered trade mark of
Oxford University Press in the UK and in certain other countries

Published in the United States of America by Oxford University Press
198 Madison Avenue, New York, NY 10016, United States of America

British Library Cataloguing in Publication Data

Data available

Library of Congress Control Number: 2023934771

ISBN 978-0-19-886158-4

DOI: 10.1093/oso/9780198861584.001.0001

Printed and bound by
CPI Group (UK) Ltd, Croydon, CR0 4YY

Links to third party websites are provided by Oxford in good faith and
for information only. Oxford disclaims any responsibility for the materials
contained in any third party website referenced in this work.

To Hildegard and Kim

Acknowledgements

The process of writing a book often starts long before the actual 'act' of writing a book. This is certainly true for this book, which is a culmination of ideas and projects that I began developing at the very start of my PhD studies at the University of Cambridge in 2013.

My mentor, friend, and former PhD supervisor at Cambridge, Ha-Joon Chang, has been influential in shaping my intellectual journey since that time and continues to be a source of inspiration. In addition to numerous conversations and collaborative projects that have benefitted my work, Ha-Joon has provided detailed and useful feedback on this book manuscript. Ha-Joon also organized a reading group session with his current and former students to discuss my book manuscript, which ended up being incredibly useful in the final stages of writing.

Ha-Joon's work caught my interest way before we met. The very first popular science book I read during my undergraduate studies in economics in Norway was *Bad Samaritans*, one of Ha-Joon's books. During my studies, my classmate, Per Martin Sandtrøen (now a member of the Norwegian Parliament), and I were frustrated that we were being drilled in reproducing obscure mathematical models rather than learning about real-world economics. By our second year, in 2008/2009, we were yearning for alternatives to mainstream economics. That's when one of our more radical professors, Rune Skarstein, recommended *Bad Samaritans*, a book that offered precisely what we were craving. In the spring and summer of 2009, Per Martin and I talked about little else than that book. My journey into the world of development economics and political economy had begun, and there was no turning back.

This book project has also benefited greatly from numerous conversations with friends and classmates that started during my PhD studies in Cambridge. They include: José Miguel Ahumada, Pierre Bocquillon, Jack Clearman, Roman Linneberg Eliassen, Vincent

Hardy, Anne Henow, Muhammad Irfan, Jens van't Klooster, Ming Leong Kuan, Samer Kurdi, Amir Lebdioui, Vasiliki Mavroeidi, Jim Miller, Natalya Naqvi, Albert Sanghoon Park, Ivan Rajic, Jaime Royo-Olid, João Silva, and Jack Wright.

My time spent in Ethiopia—mainly during my PhD studies—has also been integral in shaping this book. While the book isn't about Ethiopia, my work there involved countless conversations with policymakers/managers/businessowners, factory tours, and visits to industrial parks, all of which helped me to gain a deeper understanding of the practical hurdles involved with catch-up industrialization and economic development. It also gave me a better insight into the challenges involved with integrating into the world economy from the perspective of a low-income country that is growing rapidly. I am grateful to numerous people in Ethiopia (many of whom I mention by name below) who took time to talk with me and facilitate meetings for me.

After I finished my PhD in 2017, I took up a postdoctoral research position at the Institute for Manufacturing (IfM) in Cambridge. This was a huge disciplinary jump for me as I was now becoming part of the Department of Engineering at the university. The IfM is an institute unlike any I have come across within the halls of academia. It is a place where social scientists and engineers meet to figure out how manufacturing is shaping society and the economy (there are, of course, engineers there who actually 'make' stuff too). Two colleagues in particular, Carlos López-Gómez and Eoin O'Sullivan, have helped refine and sharpen my thinking on industrialization, technological clusters, and the role of manufacturing in the economy. Eoin, who was the director of my research group, was also incredibly supportive and encouraging of this book project in its nascent stages. I still benefit greatly from brainstorming ideas with Eoin and Carlos. I also benefited from collaborative projects and conversations with other colleagues at the IfM, including Jennifer Castañeda-Navarrete, Katharina Greve, Jae-Yun Ho, David Leal-Ayala, Michele Paladino, Hyunkyu Park, Jaime Bonnin Roca, Thomas Coates Ulrichsen, and Sarah Wightman.

Since 2020, I have been fortunate enough to spend more time on teaching-related activities—something that motivates and inspires me—especially during my stint as Fellow at the Department of International Relations at the London School of Economics and in my current role as Assistant Professor at the Department of Politics and International Studies at Cambridge. My students have challenged me to think outside the confines of my academic niche and helped me to identify pressing economic and social issues of our time. For that, I am incredibly grateful. I can only hope that I add as much value to their education as they have to my research and this book.

Many friends and colleagues have generously offered their time to read through the book manuscript and have offered valuable feedback that has greatly improved the book. They include Baptiste Albertone, Fadi Amer, Antonio Andreoni, Guendalina Anzolin, Lorenzo Cresti, Keno Haverkamp, Mateus Labrunie, Florian Schaefer, and Ilan Strauss.

Although formal conversations and written feedback is important for improving and honing academic work, many of the ideas that came to life in chapters, sections, or subsections of this book grew from casual conversations with friends. Some of these friends include Ole Aars, Mohamed Abdelmeguid, Simon K. Andersson-Manjang, Tanuja Bhamidipati, Joakim Bjørkhaug, Jens Firman, Bogdan Ganchev, Anders Helseth, Jemma Henderson, Sophie von Huellen, Karl Petter Høyning, Eric Lautier, Aftab Malik, Giovanni Occhialli, Lee Robinson, Per Martin Sandtrøen, Miljan Sladoje, and Louis Tiao. Such ideas also grew from conversations with members of my family, including Lina Flo Hauge, Kaja Flo Hauge, Rune Løhr Hauge, and Kari Flo.

Similarly, informal conversations with colleagues and other researchers that did not limit themselves to discussing my book have often fed into the book in important ways. These conversations often came to life at dinners, workshops, conferences, and even sometimes on Twitter. This includes conversations with Maha Abdelrahman, Matthew Alford, Tilman Altenburg, Carolina Alves, Karishma Banga, Pritish Behuria, Lukas Brun, Brendan Burchell, Reda Cherif, Christopher Clapham, Diane Coyle, Chris Cramer, Chris Foster,

Shailaja Fennell, Goitom Gebreluel, Gary Gereffi, Jeremy Green, Nobuya Haraguchi, Fuad Hasanov, Jason Hickel, Roberto Iacono, Kyunghoon Kim, Keun Lee, Guanie Lim, Sarah J. Lockwood, Laura Mann, Jörg Mayer, Kate Meagher, Belachew Mekuria, Khaled Nadvi, Arkebe Oqubay, Carlos Oya, Christian Parschau, Helena Pérez Niño, Annalisa Primi, Pseudoerasmus, James Putzel, Joeva Sean Rock, Sonja Schaefer, Lukas Schlögl, Nicolai Schulz, Adnan Seric, Jason Sharman, Jewellord Nemh Singh, Cornelia Staritz, Howard Stein, Andy Sumner, Nahom Teklewold, Kasper Vrolijk, Robert Wade, Lindsay Whitfield, Michael Woldemariam, and Nimrod Zalk.

This book project kicked off for real after I sent an email to Adam Swallow at Oxford University Press (OUP) outlining some ideas for a book. I am grateful for his encouragement to pursue these ideas and to formally submit a proposal. Other editors at OUP have also been very helpful and supportive throughout the book-writing process. I would like to mention Vicki Sunter in particular, who responded to dozens of queries in a flash and provided me with clear, detailed, and useful information as the book approached the production stage. I would also like thank anonymous reviewers who provided useful feedback on the book proposal and the manuscript.

The incredible artwork for the book's cover was completed by the talented artist and friend, Sumera (Sumi) Azharuddin. It was a pleasure working with Sumi, who patiently listened to all my strange ideas for the artwork and made my vision come to life.

I am forever thankful for the two members of my little family who are around me every day: my wife, Neeraja, and our cockapoo, Zelda. They are the foundation of my support system. Writing a book is at times lonely and stressful, but Neeraja and Zelda are there to fill every day with love, laughter, and play. Neeraja has also offered crucial support and advice on the book. She has read and edited the entire book manuscript, she has always been available when I asked for help with the book (whether it's about improving a paragraph, heading, or figure in the book), and she has patiently offered emotional support through my highs and lows throughout the book-writing process. She has done all these things while being in a full-time job that's more demanding than mine. It's difficult to see how this book could have been written without Neeraja. Zelda, although unable to provide feedback on the book, makes sure that I don't forget about the important things in life: cuddles and play. Our walks in Hampstead Heath help me unwind and keep my mind sharp for when I need it. She often crawls up on my lap when I work and was in fact sitting or sleeping in my lap for a significant chunk of the book-writing process. While I can't say this made me more productive, it certainly made the experience a lot more wholesome.

Finally, I would like to mention my father and mother. My late father, Kim Hauge, inspired me to understand and explore the world beyond Norway, especially by sharing his stories of working as a physician in the Middle East and East Africa in the 1980s. My mother, Hildegard Löhr, helped me to develop a love for academic and intellectual endeavours by taking me on journeys through books, places, and puzzles. She has made me into the person I am today. She also shows unwavering support and interest in my academic work and has consistently nudged me to focus more on environmental issues in my research. I dedicate this book to Hildegard and Kim.

Contents

List of figures

Introduction

About 250 years ago, something spectacular happened to the way we make things. We started using machines on a large scale. We have always been manufacturing things, transforming raw materials into finished products, but before the late eighteenth century, people around the world mostly manufactured things using hands and basic tools rather than machines. The introduction of machines transformed society. Mechanization and the clear separation of tasks between workers enabled rapid productivity growth: each worker was able to produce more output per hour. We saw the rise of different 'industries', including the textile industry, the iron industry, and the glass-making industry. This became known as the *Industrial Revolution*. It started in Great Britain and marks a major turning point in history. Almost every aspect of daily life was influenced in some way. Because of productivity growth, economic output grew considerably and so the standard of living for most people improved. For the first time in history, it continued to improve consistently.

Different technologies and inventions were crucial in driving the Industrial Revolution, such as the steam engine, machine tools, and the power loom. However, these technologies came together in a single physical space where workers operated them in a system of distinct division of tasks: the factory. The factory stood at the centre of this turning point in history. The rise of the factory system also changed the world economy. Some countries started surging ahead economically and technologically at a pace never witnessed before. Today, if we look back at countries that have successfully embarked on this transformation (from poor to rich, from low-income to high-income, from developing to developed), we will see that they have applied a mix of different ingredients to create a winning formula. But the main ingredient has always been the same:

The Future of the Factory. Jostein Hauge, Oxford University Press. © Jostein Hauge (2023).
DOI: 10.1093/oso/9780198861584.003.0001

industrialization. More specifically, countries that have undergone this transformation have strengthened their capabilities in manufacturing and factory-based production, relinquishing dependence on unprocessed agricultural goods and natural resources. Industrialization has come to be seen as the foundation of technological progress, innovation, international competitiveness, and rapid growth in productivity and economic output. This is why the terms 'industrialized countries' and 'developed countries' are often used interchangeably today.

This long-established relationship between economic prosperity and industrialization is now starting to change. 'Megatrends'—trends within the domains of technology, economy, society, and ecology that have a global impact—are changing the way countries develop their economies, they are changing traditional ideas of technological progress, and they are changing the feasibility of traditional industrial policy. In a nutshell, they are shaping 'the future of the factory'. Four megatrends in particular are worth paying attention to:

(1) *The rise of services*: oddly, most of today's industrialized countries do not have much industry at all as measured by their manufacturing output. In fact, over the past few decades, almost all regions in the world have experienced a decline in manufacturing output and a rise in service output as a share of total economic output. Services now represent more than 60% of world gross domestic product (GDP). The world's largest and most profitable companies, like Amazon, Google, or Walmart, hardly manufacture things. Even some of the world's most profitable manufacturing companies (i.e. Apple, Samsung, Toyota, and Volkswagen) get most of their profits from activities classified as services, such as research and development, industrial design, retail, and marketing. Many countries in the global South are now riding on the back of service-led growth, including India, Kenya, the Philippines, and Rwanda. What explains the rise of services? A big part of the explanation is developments in information and

communication technology (ICT), which have made productivity growth more easily achievable in a range of services and have increased the potential of services to have positive spillover effects to the rest of the economy. We are witnessing this especially in services that use digital technology (e.g. financial services and consulting services) or are themselves digitalized, as in software development services. Services have also become a more important part of international trade. In this area as well, the main driver is technological advances in ICT. Thanks to the rise of the internet and the decline in the cost of phone calls, many services can now be delivered more easily over long distances. The cost of trading services has, in many instances, come down to a level comparable to the cost of trading manufactured goods. The rise of services challenges the established view that the manufacturing sector is the source of productivity growth, innovation, and trade.

(2) *Digital automation technologies*: there are growing concerns that artificial intelligence (AI)-related technologies will enable automation and technology-induced job displacement at a pace we haven't seen before. Not many years ago, computer-based automation was limited by the need to be able to describe/codify every operation that needed to be done. This made it difficult for automation to be used in applications which involve abstract thinking, manual adaptability, and/or situational awareness in both high-skilled jobs (like creative design) and low-skilled jobs (like housework). It is believed that rapid advances in AI and in other technological domains associated with the so-called fourth Industrial Revolution—such as the miniaturization of computers, increased computing power, and continuous data collection through the internet-of-things—will make automation more widespread. Considering what this book is about, the roll-out of new, digital automation technologies warrants special attention because many studies suggest that jobs in the global South are at higher risk of automation, especially routine jobs in the manufacturing sector or the job-creating potential

of the manufacturing sector. The prospect of automation-related unemployment is, in fact, fuelling arguments that manufacturing-led growth and traditional industrialization is under threat and that many countries must therefore look for new development models and new ways of creating jobs.

(3) *Globalization of production*: a fascinating part of the era of globalization we are living in now is how production systems have become increasingly fragmented and how tasks and activities within these production systems have dispersed globally. This has led to complex and global networks of firms, popularly referred to as global value chains, global production networks, and/or global supply chains. Think about how and where an iPhone is made today. The iPhone is officially made by Apple, but Apple itself doesn't actually have any factories that play a major part in making the iPhone. Although Apple plays a big part in retail, design, and marketing activities, the company offshores the actual production of the iPhone to several other companies, examples being Toshiba, Samsung, Intel, Sony, SK Hynix, Foxconn, LG, and Qualcomm. Some of these companies are based in the United States, but most of them are based in Japan, South Korea, or Taiwan. In turn, none of these companies make the entire iPhone; they all specialize in producing different parts of the iPhone, whether it be the memory chips, the display, the processor chips, the battery, or the hard drive. We have to take a step to yet another set of companies and countries to figure out who assembles the phone as assembly is normally carried out in China by various contract manufacturers, mostly based in Taiwan.[1] Complex value chains like these are not unique for the iPhone. Practically all the 'stuff' consumed today in the global North is produced by firms and workers spread across many countries in the global South. Even amidst fears of deglobalization and reshoring caused by bottlenecks in global supply chains in the wake of the COVID-19 pandemic and the war in Ukraine, the globalization of production is still going strong. This new era of globalization

presents both opportunities and challenges for industrialization in countries in the global South and also calls for a discussion on possible reforms of rules and frameworks governing international trade.

(4) *Ecological breakdown*: we are living in an age of ecological breakdown. The Intergovernmental Panel for Climate Change (IPCC)[2] has explicitly stated that human influence, mainly through the emission of greenhouse gases in energy use, has warmed the climate at a rate we haven't seen for several thousands of years. Global warming is only one part of ecological breakdown though. Another part of ecological breakdown that does not receive as much attention is the plunder of our planet's resources (resource use, in scientific jargon). Think about all the stuff that's extracted from the earth, like plant-based material (biomass), fossil fuels, metals, and non-metallic minerals. Even if we are able to mitigate global warming (e.g. by switching fully to clean energy), this does little to reverse deforestation, soil depletion, overfishing, unsustainable extraction of metals and minerals, and mass extinction of species, which all have more to do with the constant growth in material output. Ecological breakdown is a central challenge to industrialization and manufacturing-led growth strategies. The nature of industrial production and capital accumulation since the first Industrial Revolution have involved unprecedented greenhouse gas emissions and extraction of the earth's resources. International climate agreements even have benchmarks to compare today's levels of global warming to 'pre-industrial levels' because this is the last time we can confidently say that we lived within planetary boundaries. Although we have seen efforts, in recent years, to make production and consumption greener, the rate of expansion combined with expectation of more growth has not slowed down the ecological toll of industrialization and manufacturing-led growth. In the age of ecological breakdown, we need to more honestly discuss whether there are contradictions and trade-offs between industrialization and

ecological sustainability. When thinking about policy implications, we need to explore the possibility of giving some countries more 'ecological policy space' than other countries, given how national responsibility for ecological breakdown is highly unequal across the world.

In this book, I analyse how these four megatrends are changing industrialization and how they call for new thinking about industrialization, providing some insight into 'the future of the factory'. Based on this analysis, I chart new pathways for industrial policy and global governance.

It will become clear that some megatrends are changing industrialization less than others. For example, while countries should look to tap into services for innovation and trade, I will show how the manufacturing sector remains the backbone of economic development and prosperity. And although automation technologies are displacing jobs rapidly in some manufacturing sub-sectors, we will most likely witness a reorganization of the global labour force rather than large-scale job displacement, in line with historical trends. In this sense, the rise of services and digital automation technologies do not call into question traditional industrialization and industrial policy to the degree many people think that they are.

On the other hand, the remaining two megatrends—globalization of production and ecological breakdown—are changing industrialization by making it more challenging for countries in the global South to develop their economies. The globalization of production is exacerbating power asymmetries in the global economy in favour of transnational corporations based in the global North and decreasing profit margins for workers, firms, and entire countries in the global South. Ecological breakdown, caused by the global North, is having the most devastating impact for people and ecology in the global South and is also putting constraints on capital accumulation, productivity growth, and, hence, industrialization in the global South.

We see that, in order to understand the future of industrialization, it is not enough just to look at the role of technology through a traditional economics lens. We also need to understand the role of power and politics in the global economy. That is a very important part of this book and also one of the book's important contributions, namely, that it approaches empirical questions with a rare, but necessary, combination of approaches: from mainstream economics, on the one hand, to heterodox economics, political economy, innovation studies, sociology, and political ecology, on the other.

Approach and contribution of the book

The term 'megatrend' is a term mostly used in consultancy and business communities to describe forces that are changing, or could change, the global economy, business, and society.[3] The term serves as a useful analytical lens for this book because it is both broad and narrow at the same time. Its breadth allows the adoption of a wide scope, and, in one comprehensive text, discuss questions and issues that cut across one another but are too often found in separate books and/or in separate disciplines. The specificity of the term isn't obvious but arises once the term is applied to a specific subject of study, as with industrialization, which is the case of this book. Overall, the discussion and analysis of this subject of study becomes richer and more comprehensive through the lens of megatrends. This lens also allows new analyses and discussions to emerge and intersect. In this book, a good example of this would be the discussion on how technology, power, and politics all impact industrialization but do so differently and to different degrees.

Another motivation for making the term 'megatrend' central to the book is that it's a term that draws attention from many areas of society and helps to package academic material with more flair. One of the central aims during the writing process was to produce a book that, on the one hand, provides intellectual rigour and depth and, on the other hand, is interesting, accessible, and clear to those who are new to the debates, concepts, and ideas within the book. In this sense, the book, in addition to breaking ground intellectually and academically, provides the 'unbaptized' reader with an opportunity to be introduced to development economics, political economy, and the major shifts of the twenty-first century that are shaping the world economy. The book is therefore useful for two types of audiences. The first are those who have already developed an interest in the issues I cover, either deep or shallow, either within or outside academic communities. The second are those who have not developed an interest but are curious to learn more about pressing issues in the world economy and how they impact opportunities for economic growth and development.

There are, of course, other megatrends than the ones I discuss in this book that shape industrialization pathways. Digitalization and, more broadly, the so-called fourth Industrial Revolution may present new opportunities or challenges for industrialization in the global South.[4] The rise of China in the global economy has implications for industrialization trajectories across the world as China's industrial strategy and trade orientation has shown to have global ramifications. And it might turn out that regionalization and deglobalization become more pressing issues than the analysis in this book implies (see Chapters 3 and 4). However, there are many ways to slice the same pie. For example, with respect to the fourth Industrial Revolution, I focus on megatrends within the realm of digital technologies that I believe are the most pressing ones to discuss in debates on industrialization, namely, the rise of digital services and digital automation technologies. I deliberately shy away from the term 'the fourth Industrial Revolution' as I believe that we have not yet witnessed a fourth industrial/technological revolution but rather continuing developments and innovations in digital technologies.[5] With respect to the rise of China, this is a topic that I implicitly discuss in my chapter on globalization of production as China plays an integral part in global value chains.

In addition to a novel interpretation of how each megatrend is changing industrialization, there are two aspects of this book that markedly separates it from recent books on similar topics.[6] The first is that the net cast is wider. No previous books have provided an encompassing analysis on the role of technology, globalization, and ecology in shaping industrialization. The motivation for casting such a wide net is simply because changes and disruptions in the world economy call for it. A focus narrower than the one I have adopted in the book would leave out important issues. The second, and equally important, aspect of this book that makes it distinctly different from other books on similar topics is that it adopts a critical lens. This means that I analyse megatrends not only from the perspective of mainstream economics but also from the perspective of heterodox economics, political economy, innovation studies, sociology, and political ecology. Consequently, the main argument of this book stands in contrast to books on similar topics, which are written chiefly from the perspective of mainstream economics, especially in that I highlight how power asymmetries in the world economy have as much, if not greater, impact on industrialization pathways than new technologies in and of themselves.

The research for this book has been ongoing since 2013, when I started studying for my PhD. This does not mean that the book project was conceived in 2013 but rather that I have carried out several research projects since that time that have all shaped the book. For my PhD project, I looked at if, and how, the expansion of global value chains calls for new approaches to industrial policy in developing countries. During my post-doctorate study, starting in 2017, I became more interested in the role of services in economic growth, specifically the demarcation between manufacturing and services in production systems. I also started developing an interest in the role of digital technologies in manufacturing-led development, especially automation technologies. Lately, I have begun to look at how ecological breakdown plays into capital accumulation, productivity growth, and industrial policy. Throughout this entire time, I have always been interested in the link between industrialization and economic development and the special properties of the manufacturing sector in driving innovation, productivity growth, and international trade. I have also carried out research in, and on, different countries throughout this time, from Ethiopia and South Africa to South Korea, Taiwan, and the United Kingdom.

Thus seen, this book is not the outcome of a single project but a culmination of many projects starting at different points in time and focusing on different countries. This is important information to share in explaining the approach of the book. It implies that it is not a book focusing on a single country, evidence gathered from a single country, or even extrapolating from a collection of countries in which I have carried out primary research. Make no mistake, this type of case-study-specific research features in the book and is important for it. But it is merely supplementary to the theoretical, empirical, and historical desk-based research I have carried out, all culminating in providing a better understanding and synthesis of how the process of industrialization is, and isn't, changing. In other words, the originality of the book mainly comes from its synthesis and interpretation rather than primary case-study research, making the account as a whole distinct.

More specifically, the primary mode of analysis is comparative and historical research. The book features numerous comparisons over time and across regions that help to strengthen the causal arguments. This approach generally involves an inductive style of investigation; causal arguments are derived from empirical analysis, though not without some theoretical assumptions. Comparative-historical methods are useful when studying real-world phenomena that shape societies in different parts of the world, such as technological change, globalization, and ecological breakdown. This is because these methods can compare the experiences of countries but also allow within-case exploration. Other major methodological traditions of the social sciences generally employ only one method. Historical and ethnographic methods rely on within-case analysis, and statistical and experimental methods rely on comparison.[7] The historical aspect of this method features heavily, drawing upon a world view originating back to the nineteenth-century German historical school of economics. This school, whose methods can be found in the works of, among others, Friedrich List, Gustav von Schmoller, and Karl Polanyi, believed that history is a key source of knowledge in understanding human actions and economic matters. Its approach to research involves searching for consistent historical patterns, constructing theories to explain them, and applying these theories to contemporary problems while taking into account changes in technological, institutional, economic, and political circumstances.[8]

Structure and key arguments of the book

Apart from the introduction and conclusion chapter, the book is divided into six core chapters. Chapter 1 sets the stage with historical and theoretical context. In that chapter, I discuss in greater detail how industrialization came to be seen as the engine of economic development, both with reference to industrialization experiences and with reference to key thinkers who developed important theories to explain the special relationship between industrialization and economic development. In Chapter 1, I also discuss the role of the state in pushing for a structural transformation of the economy, that is, rationales for industrial policy. Chapters 2–5 are the megatrend chapters. In each of these chapters, I look at how a specific megatrend is shaping, changing, and calling into question traditional industrialization: Chapter 2 is about the rise of services, Chapter 3 is about digital automation technologies, Chapter 4 is about the globalization and deglobalization of production, and Chapter 5 is about ecological breakdown. Whilst writing the megatrend chapters, I deliberately shied away from policy implications, that is, the 'So what?' question. The reason for this is because I have written a separate chapter addressing policy implications, namely, Chapter 6. In this chapter, I outline six policy pillars that form a foundation for reforming and designing policy based on the preceding analysis in the book, focusing mostly on industrial policy. Four out of the six policy pillars are linked to their respective megatrend, while two policy pillars are of a more general nature.[9]

Each chapter can be read independently of one another—a deliberate choice I made during the writing process. For readers that don't have prior knowledge of topics covered in the book, the one chapter that might be challenging to read without having read any of the other chapters is the chapter on policy implications (Chapter 6). Because of this (and because we live in an age where the amount of information we are asked to process on a daily basis is so vast that not many people will find the time to read a non-fiction book cover-to-cover), each megatrend chapter comes with a summary written as a condensed version of the chapter. This means that there are many ways to quickly obtain the key analysis and takeaway messages of the book. I advise readers with limited time to skim through only the introduction and conclusion chapters. Readers that have a bit more time can read these in combination with the summaries of the megatrend chapters and a chosen combination of the policy pillars in the policy chapter (just like the megatrend chapters, the policy pillars can be read independently of one another). And I promise that those who read the book cover-to-cover will strengthen their knowledge on the role of industrialization in economic development and how big, global trends are changing and shaping industrialization pathways.

At the beginning of this chapter, I outlined the megatrends that are shaping and changing industrialization, but I did not say much about the key arguments and conclusions arising from my analysis of these megatrends. So let me give the reader a taste of the book's key arguments.

The first takeaway message of the book is that technology is having a smaller impact on industrialization pathways than generally thought. I am thinking of technology in a direct and explicit sense here, specifically concerning the rise of digital services and digital automation technologies. I will show how digital services, although increasingly an avenue for economic development, is not replacing manufacturing as the engine of innovation and economic development. And I will show how digital automation technologies, although disruptive in some sectors and some countries, is not a significant threat to job displacement in the manufacturing sector. Don't get me wrong: these developments are, of course, having a big impact across the world. But we have excessively hyped up the expected impact of new technologies on economic organization, as we have done so many times in the past. Traditional industrialization and factory-based production remains crucial for economic development and innovation.

The second takeaway message of the book is that power asymmetries in the world economy are creating uneven opportunities to reap the benefits from industrialization. At worst, global power asymmetries make it harder for countries in the global South to industrialize altogether. We need to pay more attention to power, politics, and uneven development at the global level in order to see how the gains from growth are distributed. Looking at economic growth, development, and industrialization with an international and political lens, you will see that industrialization is a competitive game that involves power, politics, dirty play, and even warfare. It involves firms and sovereign states competing against one another to gain a competitive edge, economically, militarily, and technologically.

In any competitive game that has no clear end, players not only strategize to get to the top of the podium but also strategize at how power can be wielded to stay on top of the podium once they get there. A few select countries in the global North have climbed to the top of the podium during past few centuries, starting with the European colonization of the world. This type of colonization no longer exists, but countries and firms in the global North still wield the power they have amassed in any way they can to stay on top of the podium. Transnational corporations based in the global North are more powerful than ever, and they often use this power to prevent countries, firms, and workers in the global South from getting a fair share of profits in global production systems. They also use their power to lobby for international trade agreements to work in their interests. Additionally, countries in the global North refuse to take their fair share of blame for ecological breakdown, preaching green industrial policy to countries in the global South before putting their own house in order. In a sense, the global North has colonized our ecological commons and show no signs of wanting to decolonize it.

The implications for industrial policy and international politics are different once power asymmetries and uneven development in the world economy are recognized. Admittedly, we should not dismiss the autonomy and ability that countries in the global South have to successfully implement industrial policies in the twenty-first century. But we also need to step into the realm of international political economy when we discuss industrial policy for the future. That's why, in this book, in addition to suggesting new pathways for domestic industrial policy based on technological change, I also talk about ways of creating a level playing field in the world economy. In this respect, I strongly advocate for reforming our system of international trade to be fair rather than 'free' and also suggest that countries in the global South should have more ecological policy space in their implementation of industrial policy.

To close the introduction, let me say something about which countries this book holds lessons for, policy implications for, and policy inspiration for. In many ways, there is something here for all countries in the world. One might think that a book about industrialization is pitched for countries that have yet to industrialize or stand to benefit most from developing industrial capabilities. This is, of course, true but only to some degree. Many of the so-called industrialized countries (i.e. high-income countries) have experienced de-industrialization and are looking to rejuvenate their manufacturing sectors. For example, in the United States, two consecutive administrations representing opposing political parties (the Trump administration and the Biden administration) have campaigned on platforms to revitalize the US manufacturing sector. In July 2022, the United States Senate passed a historical $280 billion industrial policy bill, reflecting a rare bipartisan consensus.[10] The bill aims at rebuilding and reshoring high-tech manufacturing, especially to reduce increasing dependence on imports from China.

Although high-income countries are realizing how fatal it can be to neglect manufacturing, they are also experiencing the rise of services as an avenue for innovation and productivity growth. After all, services now make up the major share of the economy in practically all high-income countries. Even in global value chains centred around manufacturing, high-income countries have started to realize that many benefits come with specializing in services like research and development (R&D), marketing, sales, and design.

In this sense, my analysis in Chapters 1, 2, and 3 contains important information not only for the global South but also for the global North: discussions around the need for (re-)industrialization, challenges and opportunities surrounding digital technology, and the role of manufacturing versus services in the economy is proving to be relevant for countries of all levels of income.

In Chapters 4 and 5 (the third and fourth megatrend), I more specifically talk about industrialization challenges in the global South in the context of uneven development and power asymmetries in the world economy. But again, these chapters tie into economic dynamics and policy formulation in countries of all levels of income. How? While domestic policy is ultimately what will shape domestic industrialization outcomes, these outcomes in the global South are greatly impacted by governance agendas and actions in the global North. As we will see in Chapter 4, transnational corporations headquartered in the global North more than ever control the fate of workers, firms, and sometimes even entire countries in the global South. And, of course, this ties into the global governance of trade—especially through the World Trade Organization, where the interests of all sovereign states, but especially the most powerful states, play a role.

In Chapter 5, which is devoted to analysing industrialization challenges in the context of ecological breakdown, development possibilities for countries in the global South is determined by actions in the global North. It is pretty clear that if countries who have little-to-no industrial capabilities are to build them up, the countries who are responsible for ecological breakdown and continue to plunder the planet for resources need to find ways to drastically reduce their material footprint and greenhouse gas emissions. Moreover, seeing that we have already entered the age of ecological breakdown, it is high time to discuss climate reparations and climate justice, given the uneven global responsibility for ecological breakdown.

Seeing that so many chapters play into economic dynamics and policy agendas in countries of all levels of income, Chapter 6, devoted to the 'So what?' question, naturally focuses on policy action

across the world. An overarching theme is policies to achieve industrialization and economic development in the global South. But in
order for this to be achieved, action needs to be taken by sovereign
states in both the global South and the global North as well as in
organizations that operate in the domain of global governance.

As the reader can tell by now, I often use a distinction between the
global South and the global North. This distinction is analogous to
that of 'developing' and 'developed' countries. However, the process
of development is not a process with a clear end so the term 'developed country' is a misleading term in my view. It is also misleading
in the sense that many so-called developed countries perform poorly
on key development indicators. The United States is a good case in
point as it is a high-income country, held by many as an economic
model to aspire to, but turns out to be underdeveloped in many ways.
In 2021, 37.9 million people in the United States lived in poverty,
according to a government census.[11] The United States also scores
poorly on life expectancy, ranking fifty-fourth in the world.[12] This
can hardly be called 'developed'. The term 'developing country' is a
term I'm more inclined to use, which mostly refers to low-income
and middle-income countries. But this term also runs into problems. Many so-called developing countries are not developing at
all or stagnate in their development process. In the past fifty years,
the incomes of today's high-income countries have, on aggregate,
been diverging from the incomes of low-income and middle-income
countries in absolute terms. So, who's really developing here?

The terms, global South and global North, are more unproblem-
atic seeing that, in a direct sense, they refer to geographic regions.
Geographically, the global North is still home to most of today's
high-income countries and the global South is still home to most of
today's low-income and middle-income countries. This also makes
these terms highly applicable for a book on economic development,
growth, and international political economy. These terms also have
a stronger link in the literature to historic relationships of imperialism, colonialism, and uneven development processes—themes
running throughout the book. However, these terms do not come
without caveats either. On the topic of globalization, I will highlight

how the global North has profited on the backs of workers, firms, and countries in the global South. But many workers in the global North have suffered from globalization as well. On the topic of ecological breakdown, I highlight that the global North, not the global South, is responsible for excess energy and resource use. A slightly more nuanced take would be that ecological breakdown has been caused by large, transnational corporations and the wealthiest people across both the global North and the global South. I try to get these nuances across throughout the book, but, at times, I cannot afford a lengthy explanation or keep repeating the same caveat. So do keep in mind that when I write about the global North almost as if it's a culprit in the world economy, I am chiefly referring to powerful transnational corporations and the wealthiest, often based in the global North.

1

Industrialization in context

History and theory

Few politicians have lived a life as eventful as Alexander Hamilton (1757–1804). Orphaned as a child in the island of Nevis in the Caribbean, he was fortunate enough to be taken in by a wealthy merchant. Through this connection, he started acquiring considerable commercial and clerking experience in the trading business in the Caribbean as early as fourteen years of age. Hamilton eventually pursued an education in New York City and went on to have a successful career in military, law, business, and politics. He served as an artillery officer and important aide to George Washington in the American Revolutionary War, founded the Bank of New York (which, today, is a massive investment bank), wrote most of the essays that served as a basis for the United States Constitution, and was appointed the very first Secretary of the Treasury (i.e. finance minister) in the United States. For his leadership role in the American revolutionary era, Hamilton is widely considered to be one of the key Founding Fathers of the United States. As if Hamilton's life wasn't eventful enough, he died in dramatic fashion in his late forties. Due to a long-standing rivalry with another prominent politician, Aaron Burr, who was serving as Vice President of the United States at the time, a pistol duel was arranged between the two men in New Jersey in 1804. In the duel, Burr fatally wounded Hamilton, who died the day after.

Most Americans today know of Hamilton. Some, of course, know of him through the history books, but most people know his name because he is depicted on all $10 banknotes in the United States. Now, Hamilton has reached global fame, and it is not because US

The Future of the Factory. Jostein Hauge, Oxford University Press. © Jostein Hauge (2023).
DOI: 10.1093/oso/9780198861584.003.0002

banknotes are widely used around the world but rather thanks to the sung-and-rapped-through Broadway musical about Hamilton's life, simply entitled 'Hamilton', created by Lin-Manuel Miranda and inspired by Ron Chernow's biography on Hamilton.[1] The musical, casting non-white actors as the Founding Fathers and described by Miranda as 'America then, as told by America now', has achieved universal acclaim.[2]

I watched this musical a few years ago—which, by the way, I highly recommend—and was surprised that there was little coverage of Hamilton's writings on industrialization and industrial policy. In retrospect, I realize that there might be more entertaining things to cover in a musical about Hamilton's life than his thoughts on industrialization. But for those interested in the history of thought on economic development, mercantilism, industrialization, and industrial policy, Hamilton is a very important figure. During his time as Secretary of the Treasury, he submitted a wealth of reports to the United States Congress that served as building blocks for the country's economic system. One that has become especially well known was the 'Report on the Subject of Manufactures' submitted to Congress in 1791. In the report, he stressed that the United States needed to develop its manufacturing sector in order to grow its economy, bolster its military, secure its sovereignty, increase productivity, and absorb labour. He also stressed that industrialization was necessary to avoid being disadvantaged in trade with European nations, especially Great Britain, the industrial superpower at the time. The way to do this, according to Hamilton, was for the United States to protect and nurture its manufacturing sector through active use of industrial and trade policy. More specifically, industrialization was to be achieved by strategically applying tariffs and import bans on imported manufactured goods.[3]

The significance of Hamilton's report cannot be overstated. It was the first sophisticated document to challenge Adam Smith's ideas on free trade, especially the Scottish thinker's advice that the United States should focus its efforts on agriculture and avoid protectionist measures in its manufacturing sector.[4] Hamilton's report helped to build support for the introduction of tariffs in the United States in the 1790s, but it was only after his death that his ideas really caught on in the political landscape. In the wake of increasing competition from British manufacturers in the 1810s, US politicians, led by Henry Clay, took up the protectionist cause with growing success. Tariffs gradually shot up, and, throughout the nineteenth century, no country in the world had higher tariff rates on imported manufactures than the United States. Hamilton's idea of strategic government intervention and protection for the purpose of developing industrial capabilities has now become a staple justification for trade protectionism and industrial policy. It is now known widely known as the 'infant industry argument'. It is one of the very first and most important rationales for industrial policy.

Hamilton's report on industrialization and industrial policy is important to remember for more than just the infant industry argument—it's also an important reminder of when, and how, thinking on economic growth and international competitiveness was changing. The late eighteenth century was a time when the Industrial Revolution started picking up pace in Great Britain. Eventually, the country surged ahead of other countries in terms of economic growth, productivity growth, material standards of living, and global economic power. Many countries, like the United States, obviously wanted to emulate Great Britain's success. Throughout the nineteenth century, the United States and many European countries succeeded in their catch-up mission. By the early twentieth century, the world had clearly become divided into two groups of economies: one was rich and industrialized, the other poor and dependent on agriculture and natural resources. Industrialization and factory-based production became seen as the alfa and omega for achieving economic growth, development, and prosperity. This is why, today, we often use the terms 'industrialized country' and 'developed country' interchangeably.

This chapter is about this story—the story of how industrialization became so closely connected to growth and development. I tell the story with reference to both the history of industrialization and the history of theories on industrialization all the way up to the late twentieth century. I also tell the story of uneven development in the context of industrialization: how the emergence of the international trading system and imperialism aided industrialization of a select few countries at the expense of development in other countries, that is, how the divide between the global North and the global South emerged. Finally, the story of industrialization is also a story about industrial policy. Why? Because when we talk about industrialization, we are talking about a fundamental transformation of the economy. This transformation obviously does not occur spontaneously without some force calling for it and steering it. Historically, an important force in this process has been the state. So, I naturally also talk about how and why governments intervene in markets for the purpose of industrialization. In essence, this chapter then serves as a foundation, both historically and theoretically, for later chapters. It explains how, and why, industrialization became so closely connected to economic growth and development, it maps out the tensions and uneven growth trajectories between countries in this process, and it provides the rationales for state intervention this process.

Industrialization, growth, and development

A brief history of industrialization

Industrialization can be understood as a process of economic and social change that transforms a society from agrarian (or dependent on natural resources) to industrial, involving an extensive expansion of manufacturing output. Most scholars who study industrialization are interested in events in the lead-up to, during, and after the Industrial Revolution. This does not mean that societies had not developed manufacturing capabilities before the Industrial Revolution. In the sixteenth and seventeenth centuries, India's textiles and China's porcelains were in demand all over the world,[5] but manufacturing production in these countries and elsewhere in the world at the time involved artisanal techniques, handicraft, and the use of basic tools; it did not involve the use of machines. Mechanized production was first introduced during the Industrial Revolution, having a transformative and lasting impact globally.

Historians do not agree on the exact starting point of the Industrial Revolution but generally agree on 1760–1830 as a date range. The seventy-year span can be explained by some historians assuming the invention of a technology as a starting point and others assuming the widespread commercialization of a technology as a starting point. The Industrial Revolution fundamentally changed manufacturing processes as well as the pace and nature of technological progress and innovation. The economic historian David Landes highlights three factors that made this technological revolution unique in the context of human history: (i) machines were able to substitute human labour and tasks in the manufacturing process; (ii) machines were able to substitute animal labour in energy production, in particular, the introduction of engines for converting heat into work, which vastly expanded the supply of energy; (iii) raw materials used in manufacturing processes, in particular minerals (like coal), became more accessible and more heavily used.[6] A few technological innovations were essential in enabling these three interdependent processes. The steam engine and subsequent innovations in steam power were essential in all aspects of the revolution and, arguably, the most important one. The first ever machine tools, including the screw-cutting lathe and the milling machine, were also important in all aspects of the revolution. The power loom and ensuing innovations in textile production gave rise to the textile industry, the very first industry to use modern production methods.

We see that many interconnected processes and innovations played a part in the Industrial Revolution. But these all came together in a single, physical space: the factory. The Industrial Revolution can therefore be understood as the rise of the factory system, where workers operated machines in a system of distinct division of tasks, giving rise to continuous productivity growth and technological change.

The Industrial Revolution enabled a pace of output expansion and economic growth in Great Britain never witnessed before. By 1820, gross domestic product (GDP) per capita in Great Britain

Country	GDP per capita, 1500 (in 1990 GK$)	GDP per capita, 1820 (in 1990 GK$)
Great Britain	762	2,122
United States	400	1,231
France	727	1,135
Italy	1,100	1,117
Germany	688	1,077
Spain	661	1,008
Portugal	606	923
Russian Empire	499	688
Japan	500	669
China	600	600

Figure 1.1 GDP per capita in the world's wealthiest countries in 1500 and 1820

Source: Author's adaptation based on data from Maddison (2007).

was $2,122, making it the unparalleled economic powerhouse of the world (see Figure 1.1). The United States was second among other large and wealthy countries, yet far behind, with a GDP per capita of $1,231. This separation between Great Britain and other wealthy countries stands in stark contrast to pre-industrial times, when levels of output per capita and income per capita were more equal between countries.

The economic and technological dominance of Great Britain became noticeable among other countries, especially because the world had become highly interconnected by the nineteenth century. Many countries made plans to catch up with Great Britain out of ambition, envy, and/or fear, and so the practice of economic and technological catch-up, imitation, transfer, and emulation became widespread. As David Landes explains with reference to Great Britain in the early nineteenth century,

This little island, with a population half that of France, was turning out about two-thirds of the world's coal, more than half of its iron and cotton cloth. Her income per capita was correspondingly higher than that of her neighbours. Her merchandise dominated in all the markets of the world; her manufacturers feared no competition [. . .] She was, in short, the very model of industrial excellence and achievement—for some, a pace-setter to be copied and surpassed; for others, a superior economic power whose achievements rested on the special bounty of an uneven Providence, hence a rival to be envied and feared. But all watched and visited and tried to learn.[7]

Eventually, the United States, many European countries, and Japan caught up with Great Britain. By 1900, Europe, North America, and Japan made up 90% of world manufacturing output, a massive improvement from only 27% in 1750.[8] Economic growth in these countries surged thanks to industrialization. Between 1820 and 1950, GDP per capita in the Europe, North America, and Japan grew at an average of 1.08% per year, compared to only 0.29% per year in the rest of the world.[9] By the early twentieth century, industrialization had become seen as synonymous with technological advancement, innovation, global economic power, international competitiveness, and military might.

Since that time, the relationship between industrialization, growth, and development has remained strong. Those countries that have transformed their economies most rapidly from low income to high income have relied heavily on industrialization.[10] The most famous examples are the so-called Asian tigers (Hong Kong, Singapore, South Korea, and Taiwan), whose pace of economic growth and industrialization between roughly 1960 and 1990 was unprecedented in history and remains so. Other countries in East Asia and Southeast Asia are following in their footsteps, examples being China, Indonesia, Malaysia, Thailand, and Vietnam. To date, no country, except a few states exceptionally rich in oil (like countries in the Arabian Peninsula) or very small financial havens (like Monaco, Lichtenstein, and many island states in the Caribbean), has achieved high and sustainable standards of living without developing an internationally competitive manufacturing sector. This is why the terms 'industrialized country' and 'developed country' are often used interchangeably.

A brief history of theories on industrialization

The concepts used in the study of industrialization are, at times, different, although connected, and deserve clarification before I go on. Some scholars are interested in economic growth (i.e. growth in output as measured by market prices) over time as a unit of study. Up until the late twentieth century, economic growth over time was practically taken as synonymous with industrialization and economic development—and is still highly relevant to the study of these variables—so, in that sense, many of these scholars are studying development and industrialization by extension. Other scholars look more specifically at technological change, innovation, the manufacturing sector, or a combination of these and economic growth/development as a unit of study. These can be different but are all related, especially in the study of industrialization. Therefore, in the paragraphs that follow, I draw on theories of economic growth, economic development, innovation, and technological change as well as industrialization.

Industrialization, growth, and development has been a primary field of study in economics dating back to classical economics in the eighteenth century. Back then, economics was known as political economy, mainly concerning itself with how nations prosper and build wealth, so this is not surprising. Adam Smith (1723–1790), who is known by many as the father of modern economics, is also known by many as the father of the political economy of growth. Smith witnessed the beginnings of the Industrial Revolution first hand and devoted a great deal of attention to analysing the economic dynamics of factories in Great Britain. In fact, the very first chapters of his magnum opus, *The Wealth of Nations*, describe the advantages of the division of labour and its relationship with the scale of activity.[11] Smith recognized that scaling up activity in factories resulted in a specialization and simplification of tasks that raised the skill of workers, saved their time, and enabled factory owners to reinvest savings more easily.[12] In other words, Smith's work was the first to detail the synergies created in the manufacturing sector between the division of labour, economies of scale, productivity growth, and capital accumulation.

Moving on to the nineteenth century, Karl Marx (1818–1883) was one of the pre-eminent scholars of technological change. While Marx was primarily interested in class conflict under the system of capitalism, he also mapped out how the interrelationship and interactions between science, technology, and human labour on the factory floor gave rise to continuous technological improvements.[13] Marx also introduced the concept of the 'capital-goods sector'. The isolation and identification of a capital-goods sector has not only given rise to useful multi-sector economic models but also furthered our understanding of the source and diffusion of technological change.[14] Another distinguished scholar of technological change in the nineteenth century was Charles Babbage (1791–1871). Babbage was a polymath, more famous for his contributions to science and engineering than to political economy: after all, he invented the very first mechanical computer. But his contributions to political economy should not be understated. His book, *On the Economy of Machinery and Manufactures*, has become influential in operations research and industrial organization.[15] Babbage based his book on dozens of visits to factories, both in Great Britain and abroad, and made a more detailed analysis of within-factory division of labour than Adam Smith. Noting that the skill level of tasks and the cost of labour could be more carefully matched in many of the factories he visited, Babbage suggested a standardization of tasks whereby high-cost workers solely focused on high-skilled tasks and low-cost workers solely focused on low-skilled task. This, in turn, would improve productivity and increase profits.

Throughout the twentieth century, the study of industrialization, growth, and development have branched out into different schools of thoughts and sub-disciplines. If you study economics at the undergraduate level today, it is not unlikely that your first encounter with the economics of growth and development will be through neoclassical economics, the dominant school of thought in mainstream economics. This would probably be through the Solow–Swan model of long-run economic growth (or some variation of it), developed by Robert Solow and Trevor Swan in 1956. This mathematically elegant model attempts to explain long-run economic growth through the forces of capital accumulation, population growth, and increases in productivity (driven by technological change). The model provides a simple way to understand important variables that influence growth, but it does not really explain growth; that is, it does not provide an analysis of the empirical drivers/sources of technological change and productivity growth. The trade-off between high-level abstraction and real-world analysis is a problem neoclassical economics has struggled with for years. The political economists Antonio Andreoni and Ha-Joon Chang provide a detailed critique of the neoclassical synthesis of growth and industrialization, arguing that it does a poor job at explaining the role of production and technology in this process.[16] A central part of their critique is that neoclassical economics maintains a 'black-box' view of production, in which organizational dynamics and technological learning over time are ignored.

Luckily, other alternatives emerged in the twentieth century that looked more deeply at the dynamics between industrialization, growth, and development. One such alternative was development economics as a distinct discipline, emerging in the years after the Second World War from the observation that some countries were lagging behind others in levels of industrialization and economic output—especially the fact that 'the rest' was lagging 'the West'. Early theories of development economics focused not only on growth but also on the special role of the manufacturing sector in development and, relatedly, structural transformation of the economy from subsistence/agricultural to modern/industrial. This included contributions from economists like (in alphabetical order) Hollis Chenery, Alexander Gerschenkron, Albert Hirschman, Nicholas Kaldor, Simon Kuznets, Arthur Lewis, Gunnar Myrdal, Ragnar Nurkse, and Raul Prebisch.[17]

Among these, the insights from Hirschman and Kaldor are worth paying special attention to when trying to understand the relationship between industrialization, economic growth, and economic development. Kaldor's three 'growth laws' are perhaps the most famous in this respect. In short, the three laws postulate that growth of manufacturing output is positively related to (i.e. causes) GDP growth (law 1) and productivity growth—both within the manufacturing sector (law 2) and outside the manufacturing sector (law 3).[18] Kaldor's points on productivity growth (laws 2 and 3) are especially important and remain remarkably relevant today. The manufacturing sector is characterized by such high-productivity growth potential vis-à-vis other sectors because it lends itself more easily to mechanization, chemical processing, spatial concentration, and technical progress. Increased manufacturing output has a positive effect on productivity growth not only within the manufacturing sector but also in other sectors. Think about how non-manufacturing sectors of the economy become more productive once the share of capital goods in those sectors increases. For example, the world's most productive agricultural sectors are heavy users of chemicals, fertilizers, pesticides, and agricultural machinery, and the world's most productive service sectors rely on top-tier computer technology, transport equipment, and, in some instances, mechanized warehouses.[19]

Kaldor's point on manufacturing-stimulated productivity growth outside the manufacturing sector leads me to a related, and important, contribution by Albert Hirschman. Hirschman argued that all sectors of the economy are linked to one another through backward and forward linkages via input demand and supply but that the manufacturing sector is characterized by stronger backward and forward linkages than other sectors of the economy, thus acting as the main engine of economic development.[20] A recent report published by the United States Manufacturers Alliance, entitled 'The Manufacturing Value Chain Is Much Bigger Than You Think!' illustrates Hirschman's point well.[21] The report uses the example of an automotive manufacturing plant, showing how it encourages the growth of a range of domestic service activities in the upstream supply chain and the downstream sales chain. The upstream supply chain includes corporate and contract research and development (R&D) services, outsourced professional services for manufacturers and distributors, transport of inputs used in production, and utilities provision for the manufacturing plant and its distribution facilities, for example, electricity, water, and gas. The downstream sales chain includes transport of manufactured goods to port or market, wholesale and warehousing operations, retail operations, and after-market maintenance and repair services of the final product. Based on this framework, the report calculates that the United States has a manufacturing value-added 'multiplier' of 3.6. This means that for every $1 of value-added in the United States manufacturing sector, another $3.60 of value-added is generated elsewhere in the domestic economy.

The economist, Joseph Schumpeter (1883–1950), constitutes a second alternative in the twentieth century to the neoclassical synthesis in thinking about growth and technological change. Schumpeter's central insight was that, in the capitalist system, innovation is a central element in driving economic growth and development.[22] More specifically, Schumpeter argued that capitalism develops through the creation of new products, new technologies, and new markets. A big reason for this, according to Schumpeter, is that entrepreneurs are highly motivated to innovate because they earn temporary monopolies and exceptionally high profits in their respective markets ('entrepreneurial profit', in the words of Schumpeter). Schumpeter's central insight that innovation is the driving force behind growth and development has also been fundamental to the idea that economic value needs to be captured (or created) in order for growth and development to happen.

Schumpeter's research has been a precursor to innovation studies, a body of work that has provided important insights into the innovation dynamics within and between the private and public sectors and their roles in shaping a country's innovation trajectory.[23] Compared to the foundations of development economics, Schumpeter and the work carrying his legacy is not as concerned with industrialization, economic catch-up, and structural transformation in the global South. But innovation studies, and scholars related to that body of work, offer useful insights into how economic growth and development happens through the process of technological change and innovation. First, this is explored in detail through the capabilities that are developed at the firm level, such as skills, procedures, organizational structures, and norms that firms utilize to create and capture value.[24] Second, scholars studying innovation systems do a better job than most other economists at detailing national structures of innovation and related productive capabilities, which, in turn, underpin important industrial policy decisions. For example, with reference to the United States economy, Gary Pisano and Willy Shih have done ground-breaking work on identifying the 'industrial commons', which they define as 'The R&D and manufacturing infrastructure, know-how, process-development skills, and engineering capabilities embedded in firms, universities, and other organizations that provide the foundation for growth and innovation in a wide range of industries'.[25] This framework has been used to show how the manufacturing sector (or the traditional idea of the manufacturing sector) is intrinsically connected—by shared capabilities and, at times, co-location—to high-value services such as R&D and industrial design. In this sense, the notion of manufacturing and services as two separate sectors, which development economists often accept, is sometimes misguided.

Industrialization, growth, and uneven development

So far, I haven't talked much about the enablers of industrialization and economic growth in Great Britain and other Northern powers apart from breakthrough innovations in manufacturing. The state, of course, was another enabler, strategically steering policy to make domestic industries internationally competitive (which I will get back to in section 1.3). A third important factor was brutal exploitation, abroad but also at home. Material standards of living improved over time in Great Britain with the onset of the Industrial Revolution, yes, but the system of capitalist production around which industrialization became organized was brutal for most working-class people. The mainstream narrative about the Industrial Revolution is that it helped to end serfdom for good—a system where peasants toiled endless hours for landowners (at times under conditions akin to slavery) in return for protection and being able to cultivate some land for their own subsistence. In reality, the Industrial Revolution and capitalist production brought people from one system of exploitation to another. Hordes of people were brought into wage-labour in factories where, again, people often toiled endless hours under slave-like conditions.

Labour was brought into factories in Great Britain through many channels. The most important ones were population growth and technology-induced unemployment (e.g., handicraft producers driven out of business and farm workers displaced by mechanical threshers and reapers). Another, somewhat overlooked, factor were the enclosures—a massive appropriation of common land which forced many dispossessed people into factories. By the end of the nineteenth century, there was almost no common land left in England, millions of dispossessed people, and therefore lots of labour available to exploit for industrial capitalists. The capitalists, of course, took advantage of all the different channels through which labour supply increased, offering workers the bare minimum in return for their labour. Labour standards were dreadful, and the first decades of the Industrial Revolution were shockingly characterized by *deteriorating* life expectancy. In some areas, life expectancy deteriorated to levels not seen since the Black Death. In Manchester, the heart of the Industrial Revolution, life expectancy fell to a mere twenty-five years, among the lowest in the country.[26]

Exploitation abroad was also a key enabler of industrialization and growth in Great Britain. By the start of the Industrial Revolution, British imperialism was well underway as the nation had already extended its global power and dominion vastly by directly seizing control of overseas territories, militarily, politically, and economically. British imperialism—and by extension, domestic industrialization—was greatly aided by its infamous East India Company, a state-supported company with a royal charter. Some say that this company is the most powerful corporation in history: at its height, it practically controlled global trade, directly colonized overseas territories on behalf of Great Britain, and shifted the global power of trade almost single-handedly from Eastern-dominated to Western-dominated. The East India Company played a crucial role in the British colonization of India. (This was one of the company's main purposes, hence its name.) It essentially became India's ruler, extracting raw materials needed for British industrialization and transferring revenues from India to the British state. The instrument of rule was coercion. The company extracted profits with physical force, it destroyed India's nascent industries, and it stole savings from India every year, every decade, for a century.[27] Industrialization in other European countries also relied on overseas appropriation of labour and natural resources through colonization. Spain extracted gold and silver from the Andes, France extracted fossil fuels and minerals from West Africa, Belgium extracted rubber from the Congo, and Portugal extracted sugar from Brazil.[28]

Colonization in its old form (between the sixteenth and mid-twentieth centuries) no longer exists. But imperialism lives on and so do imperialist trading patterns between the global North and the global South. In fact, the pattern of uneven economic exchange enforced and established during European colonization of the world between the sixteenth and mid-twentieth centuries is still going strong. Export patterns, specialization patterns, and productive capabilities are historically path-dependent and remarkably similar today when compared with the late nineteenth century, over 100 years ago.[29] Using market prices as a proxy for value, these patterns are broadly characterized by high-value goods and services produced and exported by the global North and low-value goods and services produced and exported by the global South.

The persistence of uneven economic exchange between the global South and the global North spurred theories of uneven development in the 1950s, 1960s, and 1970s—often under the rubric of dependency theory or world systems theory—arguing that the colonial pattern of exchange persists. These theories had roots in the global South, with foundational contributions especially from Latin American intellectuals (Fernando Henrique Cardoso, Celso Furtado, and Raul Prebisch) and African intellectuals (Samir Amin, Kwame Nkrumah, and Walter Rodney) but also found support among intellectuals based in the global North (Andre Gunder Frank and Immauel Wallerstein).[30] The common thread among these theories is that global capitalism has a tendency to be polarizing rather than equalizing.[31] This is explained through a number of dynamics, including terms of trade that are tilted against countries in the global South, a global economy characterized by monopoly/oligopoly capitalism dominated by corporations based in the global North, and a separation between 'centre' and 'periphery' in the world dating back to colonial times.

There is a strong case to be made for the continued relevance of theories highlighting uneven economic exchange and uneven development. More than ever, the global economy is characterized by domination of transnational corporations based in the global North (i.e. monopoly and oligopoly capitalism) who use their power and dominance to rake in massive profits at the expense of workers, firms, and entire countries in the global South. This is something I will discuss in detail in Chapter 5 of this book. Research quantifying international, uneven exchange similarly makes a strong case for the continued relevance of the abovementioned theories. A recent paper published in *Global Environmental Change* measured the physical scale of net appropriation from the global South in terms of embodied resources and labour over the period 1990–2015. It finds that the North appropriated from the South 12 billion tons of embodied raw material equivalents, 822 million hectares of embodied land, 21 exajoules of embodied energy, and 188 million person-years of embodied labour, worth $10.8 trillion in Northern prices. The paper also finds that the South's losses due to uneven exchange outstrip their total aid receipts over the period by a factor of thirty, concluding that uneven exchange is a significant driver of global inequality and uneven development.[32] One could question whether 'appropriation' is the correct word to use as the paper uses international trade flows and price differentials in international trade to measure appropriation; that is, is it simply international trade rather than appropriation? But even with the paper's shortcomings, it makes abundantly clear that exchange between the global North and the global South remains economically uneven, vastly benefiting the global North more than the global South.

The role of the state: Rationales for industrial policy

Before I present the rationales for industrial policy, let me be clear that industrial policy can fail, it has failed, and it will fail again in the future. The case for industrial policy is not an unambiguous endorsement of the state as an omniscient force that always makes the right decisions. Governments are, of course, prone to failure, corruption, and rent-seeking. The case for industrial policy is a recognition that, without a government that steers the market in the right direction, it is practically impossible transform the economy from low income to high income and/or drive the economy towards more innovative, high-value, and internationally competitive activities. In other words, industrial policy can fail, but, without any industrial policy, failure is a certainty. In the process of industrialization, the state has always played, and will continue to play, a vital role.

Some people think about the government 'picking winners' when they hear industrial policy. Others think about more technical instruments like import tariffs, subsidies for R&D, or tax breaks. Because there is no clear-cut consensus on what industrial policy looks like in practice, it is important to be clear about my take on it. I understand industrial policy as a state policy targeting specific firms and/or industries to promote the development of productive capabilities within those firms and/or industries and, by extension, promote economic development for the entire economy.[33] This kind of understanding of industrial policy covers obvious but also less obvious policy instruments and domains, including the establishment of government agencies to promote growth of specific sectors/industries, infrastructure projects, and education and training policies (to name a few). In Figure 1.2, I have created a taxonomy of policy instruments based on this kind of interpretation of industrial policy, covering five areas and twenty-five instruments. The areas are: macro-level policy, business support, trade policy, research and innovation policy, and education and training policy. This is just one of many ways of creating a taxonomy of industrial policy instruments as some areas and instruments overlap. Some people might feel that certain instruments are not specific enough (e.g. fiscal policy as an instrument has a range of sub-instruments), so let me be clear that the exact specification of areas and instruments is based on my subjective judgement.

Policy area	Policy instrument
Macro-level policy	• State-owned enterprises • Development banks or other long-term financing • Special economic zones • Fiscal policy • Monetary policy • Infrastructure investment • Price regulation • Antitrust and competition policy
Business support	• R&D subsidies and tax breaks • Assistance to small- and medium-sized enterprises • Promotion of incubators and clusters • Public–private partnerships • Promotion of venture capital • Public procurement • Optimizing firm coordination and linkages
Trade policy	• Import tariffs and quotas • Export subsidies and support • Incentives and regulation on foreign direct investment • International trade agreements
Research and innovation policy	• University research funding • Establishment of research centres and agencies • Intellectual property rights
Education and training policy	• Subsidies and tax breaks for labour training • Skills formation and upgrading schemes • International education cooperation

Figure 1.2 Taxonomy of industrial policy instruments
Source: Author, inspiration taken from Naudé (2010) and Peres and Primi (2009).

It is clear that industrial policy can take various forms and shapes, which it has throughout history. No country has replicated another's policy toolkit, but all countries that have industrialized and built up competitive productive capabilities have used industrial policy in some form or another. Ha-Joon Chang's *Kicking Away the Ladder* lays out the early history of industrial policy, showing how it played a crucial role in the industrialization of Great Britain, the United States, Germany, France, Sweden, Belgium, the Netherlands, and Switzerland.[34] The use of trade policies was especially important (import tariffs were a common industrial policy instrument in the eighteenth and nineteenth centuries) but so were direct and indirect government subsidies to support the growth of domestic industries. Even state-sponsored industrial espionage was actively used by many European countries to 'steal' technological knowledge from Great Britain during the early years of the Industrial Revolution.

In more recent times, industrial policy has become no less important. It has been well documented that the Asian tigers used a wealth of industrial policy tools during their impressive growth and industrialization spurt in the second half of the twentieth century.[35] A World Bank Report published in 1993 entitled *The East Asian Miracle*, famous for its market-endorsing account of growth among the Asian tigers, somewhat surprisingly underscores the importance of industrial policy. The report emphasizes that market-friendly policies with low price distortions and a reliance on comparative advantage was important, but it also makes a clear endorsement of industrial policy:

In each of these economies the government also intervened to foster development, often systematically and through multiple channels. Policy interventions took many forms: targeted and subsidized credit to selected industries, low deposit rates and ceilings on borrowing rates to increase profits and retained earnings, protection of domestic import substitutes, subsidies to declining industries, the establishment and financial support of government banks, public investment in applied research, firm—and industry specific export targets, development of export marketing institutions, and wide sharing of information between public and private sectors.[36]

It has, by now, become relatively uncontroversial to say that industrial policy is important for economic growth, development, and innovation. In fact, it has, in many ways, come more into fashion since the 2010s.[37] But the rationales for industrial policy are different, highlighting different types and different degrees of state intervention.

The earliest rationale for industrial policy, and arguably the most important one for developing countries, is the 'infant industry argument'. It was first proposed by Alexander Hamilton, as mentioned earlier in this chapter. The crux of his argument was that backward economies, which the United States in many ways was in the late eighteenth century, needed to protect and nurture their industries in their infancy through various policy measures (with a heavy focus on protectionism) until they attain international competitiveness.[38] Whereas Hamilton did not theorize the infant industry argument, his ideas were developed by the German political economist, Friedrich List (1789–1846), who presented a theoretical framework for the infant industry argument in his *National System of Political Economy*.[39] List, like Hamilton, believed that infant industries could not be developed without a strong, supportive government. He argued that the government had a duty to promote economic activities that could increase the wealth and power of a nation and that the promotion of such activities necessitated the protection of infant industries and jumping ahead of current comparative advantage. Both Hamilton and List are associated with mercantilism, a dominant school of economic thought in Europe from the fifteenth to the eighteenth centuries. A core pillar of the mercantilist school of thought maintains that if countries want to increase their wealth and standing in the world economy, they should look to maximize their exports and minimize their imports through the active use of industrial and trade policy.

In contemporary discussions, the rationale for industrial policy is often explained in the language of market failures. For example, when the UK Department for Business, Energy, and Industrial Strategy (BEIS) asks HM Treasury to fund a certain industrial policy instrument, it is normally asked by HM Treasury to identify the market failure that justifies the use of the policy instrument. The idea of market failures emerged within the neoclassical school of thought, most importantly through work by Arthur Cecil Pigou (1877–1959), and is an acknowledgment that there are circumstances where markets will produce suboptimal outcomes. This might sound completely obvious to some people, but a central tenet of neoclassical economics is that, other things being equal, markets will produce the most 'efficient' outcomes.

The most common example of a market failure is an externality. An externality is a consequence of a commercial activity that affects other parties without being reflected in market prices. A typical case is the environment: markets do not take into account the costs of environmental damage as a firm's production might result in environmental degradation without being reflected in market prices. This kind of environmental damage is therefore called a negative externality. However, positive externalities are more relevant to discussions on industrial policy, the classic examples being R&D and worker training. Private firms will often underinvest in R&D and worker training from a social point of view because some technological knowledge cannot be patented and because workers bring their skills with them when changing employers. In the post-Second World War period, the lack of private-sector investment in research was the principal rationale for state-funded R&D in Europe and the United States. It has also been well documented that state-funded R&D projects (particularly defence-related) made the United States' innovation system world-leading.[40]

Another important justification for industrial policy is about risk: the private sector might underinvest in risky and uncertain projects that could potentially bring high social returns in the future. Common tools/institutions to this end are state-owned enterprises and development banks. Both of these have been tremendously important in the global South as capital markets and commercial banks willing to bear the risks associated with financing ambitious industrial projects are scarce there.[41] They also have the added benefit of increased national security, economic autonomy from multinational capital, and control over strategic industries and natural resources.[42]

The twentieth century is ripe with examples of the use of development banks and state-owned enterprises in industrialization. Mexico's development bank, Nacional Financiera (NAFINSA) accounted for about twice the value of long-term loans of all private credit institutions in 1961. In Chile, between 1961 and 1970, the fixed investments of targeted projects in the industrial sector by the Chilean development bank CORFO stood at 55% of all fixed investment in industry. In 1957, the Korea Development Bank accounted for 45% of total bank lending to all industries in the country.[43] Regarding the use of state-owned enterprises, the famous examples are the industrialization periods of South Korea and Taiwan. In 1952, the state-owned enterprise sector in Taiwan accounted for 57% of industrial production.[44] It gradually declined in importance but still played an important role for a long time: between 1950 and 1980, the average investment share of state-owned enterprises in gross fixed capital formation in Taiwan was 32%, higher than that of other countries with sizeable state-owned enterprise sectors in this time period, such as Singapore, South Korea, and Brazil.[45] We have to turn to South Korea for the best example of a state-owned enterprise that grew to become a global giant. Its steel maker, POSCO, currently the fourth largest steel maker in the world, was established as a state-owned enterprise in 1968.

You should now have a good idea of the various tools of industrial policy and the rationale behind using industrial policy. But what separates successful industrial policy from unsuccessful industrial policy? Some factors are internal, as in the quality of a country's political institutions and the relationship formed between the state and the private sector. Other factors are external, such as geography, the geopolitical climate, and the state of the world economy. Entire books have been dedicated to these factors, and it is beyond the scope and purpose of this one to cover them or to offer any original synthesis of these works. One interesting answer to this question that is, however, relevant to this book, is the operational aspect of industrial policy. The late economist Alice Amsden (1943–2012), who studied industrial policy in great detail in many developing countries, suggested that successful industrial policy is characterized by *reciprocal control mechanisms*.

Reciprocal control mechanisms are in place when government support to the private sector is tied to performance. Amsden's work has provided a wealth of examples of this from countries' growth experiences in the second half of the twentieth century.[46] In Brazil, a condition for receiving soft loans from development banks was to employ non-familial professionals in positions of responsibility, such as chief financial officer and quality control engineer. In South Korea, the license to establish a general trading company depended on meeting export criteria related to value, geographical diversity, and product complexity. In Taiwan, cherry-picked firms would be granted facilities in science parks on the condition that they reinvested a certain percentage of their profits in R&D and employed advanced production techniques. In China, science and technology enterprises were granted special legal status in exchange for performance standards with respect to technically trained employment and the development of new and more advanced products.

A global intellectual perspective

Although countries across different regions of the world have records of implementing industrial policy and pursuing industrialization, one might get the idea that the intellectual and theoretical foundations of these strategies come from thinkers in the global North. However, the intellectual contributions that have fed into national economic development and industrialization strategies are geographically far more diverse than many people think, spanning the entire world.[47]

In East Asia, a region famous for successful and rapid industrialization, many scholars highlight that industrial policy has its intellectual roots outside the region. A commonly told story is that

Western neomercantilist theories, especially those of Friedrich List, were imported to Japan after the Meiji Restoration and then used in other East Asian countries in the post-Second World War era that sought to emulate Japan's industrialization.[48] List was certainly an important inspiration, but this narrative overlooks regional intellectual origins of industrial policy and trade policy. In the early Meiji years, Fukuzawa Yukichi (1835–1901), the Japanese educator, philosopher, and writer, was an important influence on economic development strategies in Japan. Although a supporter of economic openness, he favoured strategic protectionism. Fukuzawa's ideas were also admired by South Korea's head of state, Park Chung-hee, who oversaw a successful state-led industrialization push in the 1950s and 1960s emphasizing both export orientation and import substitution. In Taiwan, Chiang Kai-shek, the country's ruler from 1950 to 1975, invoked the ideas of the Chinese statesman and philosopher, Sun Yat-sen (1866-1925) as a basis for rapid industrialization. He deemed Western economic theory inferior to Chinese economic theory, stating that Taiwan's economic strategies should be grounded in Sun's philosophies, which even Taiwan's constitution declared.[49]

Earlier in the chapter, I mentioned how Latin American thinkers have been central in shaping dependency theory, a theory outlining how the world economy is characterized by a system of international trade and exchange that favours the global North at the expense of development in the global South. One of the scholars I mentioned has been central in shaping industrialization theory more broadly, namely, the Argentine economist Raul Prebish. Grounded in an analysis of price fluctuations of internationally traded goods, Prebisch argued that countries dependent on exporting unprocessed primary commodities and importing manufactured goods are hit by deteriorating terms of trade (defined as the ratio between the index of export prices and the index of import prices). This provided a strong rationale for the use of protectionist policies and import-substitution industrialization in developing countries, which, indeed, Prebisch fought for. As head of the United Nations Economic Commission for Latin America and the

Caribbean (ECLAC), he pushed for international trade agreements that would allow developing countries to retain their tariffs. Prebish's work was inspired by the Argentine economist Alejandro Bunge (1880–1943), a leading advocate of neomercantilism in Argentina in the 1920s. Prebisch's distinction between the 'core'—those countries producing and exporting manufactured goods—and 'periphery'— those countries dependent on importing manufactured goods—was reminiscent of Bunge's description of a global economy characterized by 'star' and 'satellite' countries.[50]

In Africa, especially West Africa, the ideas of Jamaican-born activist, Marcus Garvey (1887–1940) have found strong support. Garvey was a key figure in the Pan-African movement, seeking to strengthen the bonds and solidarity between people of African ancestry. Many of his ideas can be traced back to the work he did via the Universal Negro Improvement Association (UNIA), founded with Amy Ashwood (1897-1969) in 1914. After its establishment, the UNIA quickly developed branches across the world, claiming six million members globally at its height.[51] Noting that countries everywhere were strategizing for industrial expansion and conquest in the wake of the First World War, Garvey pushed for the UNIA to cultivate industrial and commercial powers in Africa and for the African diaspora. He was inspired especially by Otto von Bismarck, the first Chancellor of the German Empire, credited with unifying the various German states into a single nation. The model country for Garvey, however, was Japan. This was not only because Japan had developed impressive industrial capabilities in the early twentieth century but also because Garvey believed that Japanese imperialism could help to undermine Western imperialism.

UNIA established two high-profile economic initiatives: the Black Star Line and the Negro Factories Corporation. The Black Star Line was a shipping company tasked with establishing trade and industrial links between the black diaspora and the African continent. The Negro Factories Corporation was to cultivate manufacturing operations by, and for, all communities of African descent. Both these companies encountered economic difficulties in the early 1920s and never truly prospered. Within Africa, intellectuals also became more focused on anticolonial initiatives centred primarily around state-building. However, many African reformists and leaders were inspired by Garvey's passion for Pan-Africanism and the UNIA's strategy of using economic initiatives to challenge European imperialism in Africa. Kwame Nkrumah, Ghana's first prime minister and president, drew inspiration from the ideas of Garvey. If you've seen the flag of Ghana, you will have noticed that there is a black star in the middle of the flag. This star is, in fact, inspired by the flag of the UNIAs Black Star Line.[52] Nnamdi Azikiwe, another West African statesman and Nigeria's fist president, also cited Garvey as one of his early intellectual heroes.

Moving to East Africa, Ethiopia has a strong record of drawing on endogenous development theory. Although taking inspiration from developmental state theory with roots in twentieth-century East Asian industrialization experiences,[53] homegrown development strategies have been a pillar of the country's policy agenda for decades, if not a full century. We can, in fact, go all the way back to the early twentieth century, when the writings of Ethiopian economist and doctor Gebrehiwot Baykadagn (1886–1919) laid the foundations for Ethiopian development economics and political economy. Gebrehiwot was one of the first African intellectuals to advocate for a comprehensive programme of catch-up industrialization, and his work went on to exert considerable influence on Ethiopian development policy throughout the twentieth century.[54] His most influential book, *Mengistina Ye Hizb Astadader* (*Government and Public Administration*), was a comprehensive treatise on political economy. It outlined a detailed rationale for industrialization and industrial policy as a strategy to improve standards of living in Ethiopia and improve Ethiopia's standing in the world economy.[55]

In the twenty-first century, Gebrehiwot's legacy has carried on. Especially under Meles Zenawi, Ethiopia's head of state from 1991 until his death in 2012, development plans focused heavily on achieving productivity growth through the use of industrial policy— in both the agricultural and manufacturing sectors. Meles himself even wrote a chapter for a recent book on the political economy of development edited by world-leading economists.[56] His paper, 'States and Markets: Neoliberal Limitations and the Case for a Developmental State', provides a detailed critique of neoliberal and neoclassical economic theories, outlining how these theories fall short in explaining successful development policy and planning. Meles oversaw a relatively successful period of economic growth in Ethiopia. From 2004 to 2018, the last eight years of Meles's reign and all the years of his successor's reign, Hailemariam Desalegn, Ethiopia was one of the of the world's fastest growing economies.

The strong intellectual inclination was not unique to Meles; it was a trait that characterized the close circle that surrounded him in policy, politics, and revolutionary activities going back to the 1980s. One figure particularly worth mentioning is Arkebe Oqubay. Oqubay was not only a key political figure during Meles's tenure and during the Ethiopian liberation movement in the 1980s but also spearheaded industrial policy in Ethiopia in administrations succeeding Meles. What makes Oqubay especially worth mentioning in this context, though, are his academic contributions to political economy and development economics during his political tenure. In 2015, he published *Made in Africa: Industrial Policy in Ethiopia*, a book that details industrial policy in Ethiopia, especially since the 1990s, comprehensively weaving in the theories of development economists such as Albert Hirschman and Alice Amsden. Since the publication of this breakthrough monograph, Oqubay has co-edited a number of books on development economics, industrial policy, and economic development in Africa, with contributions from world-leading intellectuals. This has made him one of Africa's leading intellectuals in the fields of political economy and development economics.

Taking stock of this entire chapter, we see, both with reference to history and theory, how industrialization and industrial policy have been cornerstones in economic development. And we see this with reference to both theories of economic development and strategies for economic development, spanning the entire globe. It is not an understatement to say that the factory has shaped the modern world. But will it keep reshaping it? What role will factory-based production play in the future world economy, and what will industrialization look like? Do some countries stand to gain more than others from the 'megatrends' that are changing industrialization? This is where we turn our focus in the remaining chapters of the book.

2

The rise of services

You will see something puzzling if you study the economic structure of today's industrialized countries: most of them do not have much industry at all as measured by their manufacturing output. In fact, over the past few decades, almost all regions in the world have experienced a decline in manufacturing output as a share of their total economic output (see Figure 2.1). The fact that seemingly so many countries are relying less on manufacturing puts into question some of the evidence and theory that I presented in Chapter 1—which, in short, showed how industrialization and economic development have historically gone hand-in-hand.

While manufacturing's share of GDP has dropped across most of the world, the share of services has gone up, now representing more than 60% of world GDP.[1] If we think about the world's largest and most profitable companies today, these statistics make complete sense. Do Amazon, Google, or Walmart manufacture things? Hardly. And if we start digging into the balance sheets of some of the world's most profitable manufacturing companies, such as Apple, Samsung, Toyota, and Volkswagen, we will see that most of their profits come from non-manufacturing activities, including research and development (R&D), industrial design, retail, and marketing. The experiences of many countries in the global South that have been growing fast in recent years also support the hypothesis that we have entered a post-industrial society. For example, India, Kenya, the Philippines, and Rwanda are all riding on the back of services-led growth, especially digital services. The hype behind service-led growth and development is fuelled not only by the proof that services are driving innovation and productivity growth but also because services have become more tradable. The manufacturing sector has

The Future of the Factory. Jostein Hauge, Oxford University Press. © Jostein Hauge (2023).
DOI: 10.1093/oso/9780198861584.003.0003

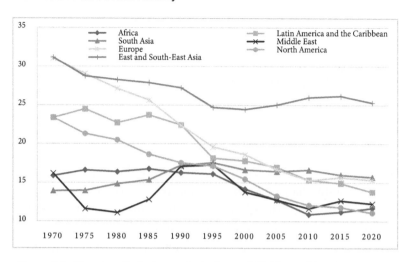

Figure 2.1 The manufacturing sector's share of GDP in world regions

Source: Author, based on data from United Nations Conference on Trade and Development (UNCTAD) Data Center.

traditionally been the bedrock of international trade, but now, a range of services is becoming an integral part of trade networks, such as distribution services, computer services, telecommunication services, financial services, and tourism.

The decline in the importance of manufacturing and the increase in the importance of services in the economy has led to a debate on whether present and future economic development trajectories will follow the traditional path of industrialization, which, most importantly, involves an expansion of the manufacturing sector. In this chapter, I take a deep dive into this debate, looking at how 'real' the rise of services is.

Services as a driver of productivity growth and innovation

The evidence

In Chapter 1, I discussed the theoretical foundations regarding the positive relationship between economic development and growth of the manufacturing sector. Some of the development economists

I mentioned, including Hollis Chenery and Simon Kuznets, actually hypothesized that following a period of industrialization, the service sector as a share of total economic output would rise and that of the manufacturing sector would fall. However, neither of these economists challenged the idea of the importance of industrialization for economic growth and development. One of first people to do so was the US sociologist, Daniel Bell. In his book, *The Coming of Post-Industrial Society*, he argued that the wealth of future societies would rely less on the production of goods and more on the provision of services and the spread of a 'knowledge class'.[2] Even at that point, he had some proof to his claim. Using data from the United States Bureau of Labour Statistics, he found that the growth in number of employees in the service sector, both in absolute and percentage terms, had been higher than that of the manufacturing sector dating as far back as 1870.

In the 1980s, shortly after the publication of Bell's book, more economists started highlighting the importance of services for economic development.[3] But only in recent years has the literature on this started to grow fast, emphasizing the increased potential of services to act as catalysts for innovation, productivity growth, and trade.[4] This is the case especially for three groups of services: (i) professional, scientific, and technical services; (ii) information and communication services; and (iii) finance and insurance services.[5]

Services have become a more important driver of productivity growth, in large part thanks to advances in information and communication technology (ICT). This group of technologies has made economies of scale more easily achievable in a range of services, increased the spillover/linkage potential of services, and made it more profitable to procure some services from specialist providers rather than provide them within a manufacturing firm.[6] We are witnessing economies of scale especially in services that use digital technology or are themselves digitalized. For some of these services, the marginal cost of providing an additional unit of service has actually come close to zero. Think about the provision of software-related services, whose characteristics are not too different from how economists are taught to think about manufacturing operations:

fixed assets are costly (e.g. server farms, cooling systems, secure sites and so on) but costs rapidly decrease with scale. The media streaming services Netflix and Spotify are two good examples, both of which are companies that can sell their services at a massive scale and low cost around the globe in a flash. In 2022, Netflix reached 220 million paying subscribers, while Spotify reached 190 million paying subscribers. A few years before that, both services only had a fraction of that number of subscribers.[7]

Analysing sector growth trends in Germany, India, the United States, and the United Kingdom (four of the world's largest economies), the World Trade Organization found that total factor productivity growth in ICT services has been higher than in the manufacturing sector in each of these four economies during the period 2005–2015.[8] Services have also become more closely linked to innovation. A common way to measure an economy's rate of innovation and technological development is to look at the volume of R&D, and there is clear evidence that R&D is focusing more on services: on a global scale, R&D expenditure in services increased from an annual average of 6.7% of total business R&D during 1990–1995 to 17% during 2005–2010.[9] A recent study on the role of US innovation within global R&D networks found that the increase in global R&D since the 1990s has been highly concentrated within ICT service operations of US-based transnational corporations.[10]

Companies providing high-tech digitalized services, examples including Netflix and Spotify, are mostly based in the global North. But there is also evidence that services in the global South are showing productivity-enhancing characteristics. Labour productivity growth in developing countries has, in fact, been higher in services than in agriculture and industry since 1990.[11] A study conducted on six low- and middle-income countries—Brazil, China, Egypt, India, Nigeria, and Russia—found that ICT services in these countries are as technology-intensive (as measured by a range of learning-by-doing and innovation metrics) as the manufacture of electronics.[12] ICT services have had a particularly positive impact in India, where the growth of such services is closely associated with the increase in economic growth since the 1980s.[13] India's total factor productivity in services grew by 2.4% between 1980 and 2006, more than twice the level of total factor productivity growth in both industry and agriculture.[14] Looking at more recent data, the World Trade Organization found that productivity growth in India's ICT services has been higher than all other economic sub-sectors—including manufacturing—every year between 2005 and 2015.[15]

Africa has also benefited, to some extent, from services-led growth. The increase in economic growth since the late 1990s in the region has been associated with an expansion of services. While Africa has experienced almost no structural change in the traditional sense, from agriculture to manufacturing, it has experienced some structural change from agriculture to services.[16] According to the United Nations Economic Commission for Africa's (UNECA's) economic report on Africa in 2015 (a report focusing on growth of services in the region), Africa's service sector grew at an annual rate of 5.8% in the period 2000–2012, higher than the world average growth rate of services.[17] The report stresses that growth of services and the growth of the region's GDP are highly correlated, although it is more careful about claiming a causal link in any direction. The growth has been strongest in ICT services (e.g. in Kenya and Rwanda), transport services (mostly airlines, like in Ethiopia) and tourism. Many of these services bring in export earnings, thereby easing severe balance-of-payments constraints in many African countries.

Scrutinizing the evidence

It is important for us to recognize the increased potential of services as a driver of productivity growth, innovation, and economic development. But it is also important that we scrutinize this evidence. We can surely attribute increased productivity growth potential to many services based on the output we see from these services, but the productivity growth is not achieved from services alone. In many digital services, technological progress and productivity growth is dependent on innovation in the manufacturing sector—think about hardware chip technologies and information transmission technologies like fibre optics and satellites. The same goes for many delivery services, which would not be as efficient without transport equipment or mechanized warehouses. Some retail and food services even implement organizational structures that originate from the manufacturing sector. For example, many fast-food restaurants use assembly techniques in their kitchens, and some even deliver food on a conveyor belt, like 'Yo! Sushi!'.[18] We can also say the same about agriculture: think about how the world's most productive agricultural economies are heavy users of chemicals, fertilizers, pesticides, and agricultural machinery.[19]

However, manufacturing activities are also dependent on services for their productivity. More or less every manufacturing firm is dependent on retail services, distribution services, utilities services, transport services, professional business services, etc. This means that manufacturing and services contribute to each other's productivity. But research on this particular topic indicates that manufacturing contributes to more value-added in the economy than services. The seminal study on this was conducted in 1989 by See-Hark Park and Kenneth Chan, who found that the manufacturing sector generates two to three times more output in the rest of the economy than does the service sector.[20]

More recent, country-specific studies make conclusions along similar lines. In France, 29% of the manufacturing workforce contribute indirectly to the production of non-manufacturing output, whereas only 13% of the service workforce contribute indirectly to the production of non-service output.[21] In Singapore, the manufacturing sector has stronger value-added spillovers to the service sector than vice versa: every 100 new manufacturing jobs are associated with 27 new non-manufacturing jobs. By contrast, every 100 new service jobs are associated with only 3 additional manufacturing jobs.[22] With respect to innovation metrics, although services are gaining ground, manufacturing still dominates. For example, in the United States (a country where manufacturing production has supposedly been on the decline since the early 1990s), the bulk of innovation still happens in the manufacturing sector: firms associated

Sector	Share of value added that is exported (US data)	Share of businesses' R&D expenditure in value added (EU data)	Share of sales to other sectors (EU data)
Agriculture	24%	0.5%	59%
Manufacturing	35%	7%	49%
Services	7%	1%	38%

Figure 2.2 The scope for trade, innovation, and spillovers of economic sectors, 2015 data

Source: Author's adaptation based on data from Nayyar et al. (2021).

mainly with industrial production still employ a majority of all scientists and engineers and the manufacturing sector accounts for most industrial R&D.[23] In fact, across both the European Union (EU) and the United States, the scope for trade, innovation, and intersectoral linkages (spillovers) is generally higher in manufacturing than in services (see Figure 2.2).[24]

We also find stronger theoretical support for manufacturing as a driver of productivity growth and innovation. In the case of spillovers and linkages, as early as 1958, Albert Hirschman theorized that the manufacturing sector is characterized by the strongest backward and forward linkages to the rest of the economy.[25] Nicholas Kaldor, in his third growth law, found that the productivity of non-manufacturing is positively correlated with the growth the manufacturing sector because of spillover effects from the manufacturing sector to other sectors.[26] It is also important to investigate the opportunities for economies of scale, which Kaldor analysed in his second growth law. In this law, Kaldor postulated that productivity in manufacturing is positively correlated with the output growth of the manufacturing sector, also known as Verdoorn's law. This is attributed to both static and dynamic economies of scale. The former refers to output level or sector size, while the latter signifies the effect of learning-by-doing, which is a function of both cumulative past output and/or cumulative production experience over time.

Economies of scale are more easily achieved in the manufacturing sector, mainly because manufacturing activities lend themselves more easily to mechanization and chemical processing compared to other types of economic activities. The ease of spatially concentrating manufacturing production is also an important factor behind the greater productivity potential. Many services have shown themselves highly resistant to productivity increases, such as health care, education, and hospitality services. The amount of time it takes for a nurse to change a bandage, a university professor to mark an essay, or a hotel receptionist to check someone into their room is the same today as it was fifty years ago. When countries become too reliant on such services, a problem arises because salaries of these professions have to rise in response to rising salaries in other sectors of the economy that have risen due to growth in productivity. This phenomenon, highlighting the dangers of becoming too reliant on 'unproductive' services, was theorized back in the 1960s by William J. Baumol and Willian G. Bowen and is known as 'Baumol's cost disease'. Baumol's cost disease also helps us to understand why countries with high manufacturing output experience higher productivity growth.[27]

The long-term evidence on economic development also offers stronger support for the manufacturing sector as a driver of productivity growth and innovation. Throughout the history of capitalism (in both the near and the distant past), more or less all countries that have transformed their economies from low to high income have done so through a process of developing their manufacturing capabilities. Between 1750 and 1950, the West's gradual establishment as the world economic hegemon—starting with the Industrial Revolution in Great Britain in the late eighteenth century—was also a process of establishing itself as the world's manufacturing hegemon.[28]

Since 1950, the pattern has hardly changed. According to a study of 'growth miracles' by the World Bank in 2008, only thirteen countries in the world have been able to sustain an annual growth rate of 7% or higher since 1950. Only two countries, both with small populations and highly idiosyncratic economic structures—Botswana and Oman[29]—are among the group of thirteen that have not grown on the basis of manufacturing-led development.[30] In a more recent study, Kaldor's growth laws have been tested in a sample of sixty-three middle- and high-income countries for the period 1990–2011.[31] The authors find that the laws are still highly valid, concluding that output growth and export growth in the manufacturing sector is essential to increasing economic growth and productivity, particularly in middle-income economies. The relationship between the growth of the manufacturing sector and sustained economic growth has, in fact, been documented as robust by many more economists.[32] Unsurprisingly, no country, except a few states exceptionally rich in oil (e.g. Brunei, Kuwait, and Qatar) or very small financial havens (e.g. Monaco and Lichtenstein), has achieved high and sustainable standards of living without developing its manufacturing sector.[33] This is why the terms 'industrialized country' and 'developed country' are often used interchangeably.

If we look in greater detail at the countries that have experienced de-industrialization, or premature de-industrialization, we see a clear trend of decelerating economic growth alongside a decline in manufacturing output. In Latin America, the region that has gone through the most severe case of premature de-industrialization, the decline in manufacturing output as share of GDP also caused a growth slow-down. In Africa, premature de-industrialization caused *negative* economic growth in the 1980s and early 1990s. Countries within the Organisation for Economic Co-operation and Development (OECD) have, on aggregate, experienced a growth slow-down alongside a decline in manufacturing production since the 1980s. In the United States, we now hear calls across political divides for rejuvenating the manufacturing sector. Both the 2016 and the 2020 presidential campaigns saw two candidates at opposite ends of the political spectrum, Bernie Sanders and Donald Trump, campaigning for a manufacturing renaissance. Shortly after assuming office in 2021, Joe Biden promised an ambitious industrial strategy for the country, a promise that he seems to be keeping.[34] Around the same time, Hilary Clinton delivered a passionate statement to Chatham House about the need for industrial policy in the United States to take back production from China.[35]

It is clear that the links between manufacturing, productivity growth, innovation, and economic development are strong. But this is not the only reason for the hype behind service-led development. Another important reason is that services are becoming a more integral part of international trade.

Services as a driver of international trade

The evidence

Thanks to digitalization, the rise of the internet, and the decline in the cost of phone calls, many services can now be delivered remotely over long distances more easily and have lowered their trade costs to a level comparable to manufactured goods.[36] Digitalization has also made services more storable, codifiable, and transferable, which, in turn, has meant that physical proximity between producers and consumers no longer constrains the scaling up of many services.[37] Taken together, these developments have considerably increased the tradability of transportation/distribution services, telecommunications/computer services (call centres or software services provided in a foreign country), financial services, and tourism.

The poster child of services-based trade success is the United Kingdom, where trade in services now accounts for around 20% of GDP (roughly 50% higher than the world average), thanks to growth in trade of mainly financial and business services.[38] India is another country that has achieved success through exporting services. It has become the world's largest exporter of ICT services, with exports in this category reaching $146 billion in 2020, a threefold increase from 2010.[39] Hyderabad, the capital of Telangana, is hailed as the prime example of services-led growth in India, where its ICT cluster has earned the nickname 'Cyberabad'. A third example is Rwanda, a country that, in the past few years, has increased its export earnings considerably through the expansion of tourism services, such as gorilla viewing. In fact, Rwanda and many other African countries, including Uganda, Tanzania, and Tunisia, report that tourism is their top single earner of foreign exchange.[40]

One of the developments in service trade we should make note is the change in the way trade in services is counted. Until recently, traditional statistics on trade in services did not cover all of the four modes of service supply, as defined in the General Agreement on Trade in Services (GATS). Most importantly, 'GATS mode 3'—commercial presence in another country (i.e. the supply of services through foreign affiliates)—had been left out. The World Trade Organization's annual flagship report published in 2019, *World Trade Report: The Future of Services Trade*, uses a new experimental data set that includes GATS mode 3.[41] According to the report, GATS mode 3 accounted for 59% of trade in services in 2017. The data presented in the report is therefore a very important contribution to understanding the changing nature of trade in services. Using the new estimates, world trade in services was worth US$13.3 trillion in 2017. This is vastly different from sources that do not include GATS mode 3. For example, the World Bank reports that trade in services in 2017 was worth US$5.4 trillion.[42] To be clear, both numbers indicate a rise in service trade over time, both in absolute numbers and as a share of world trade. But they tell a vastly different story with respect to the importance of service trade in world trade. Using 2017 figures, world trade in services reached only 28% of the value of world trade in goods (merchandise trade) according to the World Bank data. However, according to the new World Trade Organization (WTO) data, world trade in services made up 70% of the value of world trade in goods. This is a massive difference.

Although high-income countries still dominate trade in services, developing countries gained over ten percentage points in their share of world trade in services from 2005–2017 according to the abovementioned report by the WTO. This was primarily due to growth in service exports through foreign-controlled affiliates (GATS mode 3) in construction services, financial services, business services, distribution services, and digital services. This growth is highly concentrated in China and India, and the share of least developed countries in this growth is negligible. Some additional highlights from the report, using the GATS mode 3 data set are: in the period 2005–2017, the growth of world trade in services has been higher than the growth of world trade in goods; since the mid-1990s, service-sector employment as share of global total employment has steadily been increasing; and services make up an increasing share of world exports in terms of value-added. This last point is important, especially as it relates to the role of services embedded in manufacturing processes. Using a global value-chain framework in a sample of thirty-one advanced economies (mostly OECD economies), a recent study finds that services account for 37% of the value of exports by manufacturing firms.[43] The study also finds that, across these countries, between 25 and 60% of employment in manufacturing firms is found in service functions such as R&D, engineering, transport, logistics, distribution, marketing, sales, after-sale services, IT, management, administration, and back-office support.

According to the WTO's report, these are the five categories of service activities that dominate international trade today, as measured by their share of world trade in services: distribution services (19.9%); financial services (18.6%); telecommunications, computer services, audio-visuals (13.2%); transport services (11.8%); and tourism services (7.8%). These numbers also reflect the change in counting service trade as the two categories of services that constitute the highest share of world service trade—distribution services and financial services—take place predominantly by means of establishment of a commercial presence in another country (GATS mode 3).

Of course, there are still many services that, for the most part, need to be delivered locally—getting a haircut, staying at a hotel, eating at a restaurant, receiving medical treatment, and receiving an education, to name a few. But even in these areas, we are starting to see transformations. For example, medical information is accessible to anyone with an internet connection anywhere in the world, and some medical procedures, such as diagnostics and analyses, are increasingly performed remotely. Similar trends can be seen in education, with the proliferation of e-learning platforms such as Moodle and Massive Open Online Courses (MOOCs). Moreover, when we include service supply by foreign affiliates as part of service trade, many of the services that we think of as non-tradable are suddenly tradable, for instance, using a hotel service (think about Airbnb) or taking a taxi (think about Uber).

Scrutinizing the evidence

The inclusion of GATS mode 3 is a huge step in the right direction towards properly counting trade in services, but it invites a number of challenges as well. First, the WTO's 2019 report is unclear on a few important points. Let us revisit the definition of GATS mode 3, which is *commercial presence in another country*, that is, the supply of services through foreign affiliates. An important question arising from this definition is which country actually retains the economic development benefits and productive capability benefits of the activities of the foreign affiliates? This is not easy to think about in an abstract sense, so let us think about it in the context of a Norwegian construction company building a hotel in Sweden. If the Norwegian construction company builds a hotel in Sweden but uses all inputs from Sweden and all-Swedish (or other European) people to build the hotel, how much does this contribute to the Norwegian economy? One could perhaps argue that some of the technological knowledge comes from Norway and some of the managerial people are Norwegian but not much more. There seems to be a shared benefit between Sweden and Norway.

Another important question is: what exactly is counted as trade in services by foreign affiliates? In the case of the Norwegian construction company operating in Sweden, what would be counted as trade in services from Norway to Sweden? The repatriation of profits? The revenue or profits of the Norwegian company in Sweden? Another issue that invites more challenges to counting this new form of service trade is that some middle-income countries, including India, export services through foreign affiliates from high-income countries established in their own country—think about foreign affiliates from the United States operating in India. When India exports these services, do they no longer count as Indian exports but rather exports from the United States? Additionally, does GATS mode 3 create problems of double counting with respect to foreign direct investments? Last but not least, if GATS mode 3 is included in service trade, should it not also be included in goods trade?

The reason these questions are so important to ask is because when GATS mode 3 is included in service trade, the value of world trade in services more than doubles. With the inclusion of GATS mode 3 in calculations, trade in services as a share of total world trade in 2017 was 59%. Without the inclusion of GATS mode 3 in calculations, trade in services as a share of total world in trade in 2017 was 24%, which represents a negligible increase over the past few decades. It would not be an exaggeration to say that figures on service trade *without* the inclusion of GATS mode 3 would make a weak case for the tradability of services, but figures on service trade *with* the inclusion of GATS mode 3 in calculations would make a strong case for the tradability of services. With all the unanswered questions and measurement issues that the inclusion of GATS mode 3 in service trade calculations raises, I would advise against using GATS mode 3 in such calculations.

Another piece of evidence that should caution countries against relying too much on services for international trade is how strained the trade balance is for countries that have not built up a strong manufacturing sector. A quick look at the World Bank's World Development Indicators reveals that countries with the largest trade deficits are countries that have lost their manufacturing capabilities and started specializing in services, such as India, the United States, and the United Kingdom. On the other hand, countries with the largest trade surpluses are mostly countries with a strong manufacturing sector, including China, Germany, Italy, Japan, and South Korea.

The value-added of services and manufacturing: Measurement issues

Many of us don't give a second thought to the way in which economic activities are broken down into different categories. But we should, at least if we want to understand what type of activities generate economic value in the economy. Countries have ways of doing this in their systems of national accounts, and in most parts of the world, economic activities are broken down into three big categories: agriculture, manufacturing (or industry), and services. This classification invites problems, not because it does not make sense in its entirety but rather because some activities do not fit neatly into one category. And in recent years, some of the 'borderline' activities have started to generate a lot of economic value, especially those that border between manufacturing and services.

If we think about the definition of manufacturing, this should not come as a surprise. At the most basic level, manufacturing can be understood as the transformation of raw materials into finished products. At a more detailed level, it becomes clear that manufacturing is a series of interrelated activities. The central value chain of a manufacturing operation typically consists of R&D, design, production, distribution, and after-sale services. This value chain needs timely provision of technical services, like analysis, testing, and logistics. It also needs timely provision of specialist professional services, like regulatory services, intellectual property services, investment services, and consultancy services. And it needs reliable supply of materials, components, and other manufactured inputs, such as machinery, equipment, and tools.[44]

Clearly, with this systems perspective in mind, manufacturing operations encompass a range of services. But in most countries' national accounts, these manufacturing-related services are categorized as services, not as manufacturing.[45] If we want to have a true understanding of the value of manufacturing in the economy, these manufacturing-related services should be classified as manufacturing, not services. While it could, and should, be debated which services are truly 'embedded' in manufacturing, studies have made it abundantly clear that services are becoming an increasingly important part of manufacturing. According to Penny Bamber and colleagues at the Duke Global Value Chains Center, more than one-third of the value of manufacturers' exports (globally) come from services embedded in manufacturing. They find that distribution and business services make the largest contribution.[46] The EU tops the list of 'servitization' of manufacturing, where embedded services accounted for 40% of manufacturers exports in 2011.[47]

As a result of this development, some scholars suggest that policies and initiatives to promote manufacturing should take a value- chain perspective; that is, manufacturing statistics should include pre-production services, including R&D and industrial design, and post-production services, such as repairs and sales. A recent paper published by the Brookings Institutions compared employment in US manufacturing between a value-chain perspective and a nonvalue-chain perspective. They found that in 2002, manufacturing narrowly defined employed about 15.2 million workers but that the entire value chain employed nearly 37.2 million workers. By 2010, employment had dropped to 11.5 million in production and to 32.9 million across the value chain. In other words, there was de-industrialization but barely in the service segments of the value chain.[48] I have carried out a similar study but looking at value-added rather than employment. And I found similar results. I broke down the value chain of three iPhones released between 2010 and 2018 and found that manufacturing activities, narrowly defined, made up 44% of the final retail price, on average. However, a significant chunk of the remaining 56% of the value was made up of manufacturing-related services, such as R&D industrial design.[49]

Together with Eoin O'Sullivan, I have carried out a more granular study than the one on the iPhones, looking at the life science industry in the United Kingdom.[50] The UK Office for Life Sciences has undertaken a very useful exercise, mapping the landscape of the UK life science industry (medical technology and biopharmaceutical sectors) in a way that includes the range of services linked to the manufacturing process. Part of the motivation for carrying out such an exercise is that the standard way of classifying industries in the national accounts does not fully reflect the way in which the industry is really organized, especially regarding the deep links between manufacturing and service activities. We looked at all the data gathered by the Office for Life Sciences at the firm level and found that a significant share of the industry's value is generated by services: especially information and communication services; professional, scientific, and technical services; administrative and support services; and wholesale and retail trade services. In fact, the entire life science industry generates roughly three times more revenue than the core manufacturing activities in the industry. This is not to suggest that the life science industry is three times larger than the official statistics suggest or that all these service activities should be counted as manufacturing. But the industry is certainly larger than the statistics on only manufacturing suggest. And there is a case for at least including professional, scientific, and technical services in the equation. Research has made it abundantly clear that such services are closely intertwined with the manufacturing process in many industries, both geographically and through shared capabilities.[51]

There is a related measurement oddity in countries' national accounts which should make us question the evidence behind de-industrialization: the fact that the declining share of manufacturing in economic output is, in some part, due to reclassification of economic activities rather than an actual change in productive structures. In the list of economic activities in the Standard Industrial Classification (SIC) codes made by the Office for National Statistics in the United Kingdom, companies are classified according to the activity in which their largest number of employees is engaged. This means that a company that both makes and delivers a product will be classified into either manufacturing or services, not both, depending on the number of people working in each category.

The UK's *Manufacturing Metrics Review Report* from 2016 uses the example of ABC Computers Ltd, a company that employs thirty-five people, twenty of whom are employed to make computers and fifteen to deliver computers.[52] This company ends up being classified in the manufacturing category even though it employs almost half of its workforce in a non-manufacturing activity. However, if ABC Computers Ltd outsources the delivery of its products to a delivery company in the same country, there is suddenly an increase in services as a share of total output in the economy without this really being the case. This outsourcing has actually been happening on a large scale in many countries in the past few years: many services that used to be provided in-house in manufacturing firms (e.g. delivery, catering, security guards, design, programming, marketing, analytics and so on) are now supplied by independent services companies.[53]

Additionally, some manufacturing companies that have not started outsourcing their service activities have instead applied to be reclassified as service firms, even though they still conduct some manufacturing. This is mainly because the manufacturing share in their total output is falling. A UK government report estimates that up to 10% of the fall in manufacturing employment between 1998 and 2006 in the United Kingdom may be due to this reclassification effect.[54] Why is the manufacturing share in these companies' total output falling relative to services though? Looking at countries going through the de-industrialization process in the 1980s and the 1990s, Robert Rowthorn and Ramana Ramaswamy argue that the main explanation for this trend—and, more generally, the trend of a relative decrease in the size of the manufacturing sector—is that productivity in manufacturing grows faster than in services.[55] A more recent study by Fiona Tregenna similarly shows that the trend of de-industrialization in some countries is happening because the labour-intensity of manufacturing declines more rapidly over time compared to services; that is, manufacturing has higher productivity.[56] As a result of this greater productivity potential of manufacturing, prices of manufactured goods have declined relative to that of services, resulting in a falling share of manufacturing in total economic output. This is an important observation: some de-industrialization is not caused by the growing irrelevance of manufacturing but rather because manufacturing is characterized by higher productivity growth potential.

In this section, I have so far mostly focused on why, and how, we need to question the way we measure and count manufacturing and services. But there is also a need to investigate the increasingly blurry boundaries between manufacturing and agriculture. The agricultural sector contains and depends on a range of manufacturing activities which aid productivity growth and value-added in the agricultural sector.[57] However, many countries do not make it clear in their national accounts whether these activities are counted as agriculture or manufacturing. For example, are companies who carry out coffee roasting and grinding registered as agricultural companies or manufacturing companies? More importantly, are fertilizer and pesticide producers, the most important inputs to raise agricultural productivity, registered as part of the agricultural sector or the manufacturing sector? The production of fertilizer and pesticides are complicated manufacturing processes that take place in factories and should, undoubtedly, be classified as manufacturing processes.

Finally, for the sake of the argument, let us, for a moment, pretend that the value of manufacturing, services, and agriculture in countries' national accounts is counted accurately. There is still one outstanding and highly important piece of evidence that should make us question the hypothesis that the world economy has undergone de-industrialization, namely, the shifting geography of manufacturing. Given that more or less all manufacturing products are traded across borders, it might just be that a minority of countries have taken over manufacturing production from the rest of the world. A recent paper actually confirms this, finding that the manufacturing sector's value-added and employment contribution to world GDP and employment, respectively, has not changed considerably since 1970.[58] The paper highlights that the impression of global de-industrialization is due to the increasing concentration of manufacturing activities in a small number of populous countries, in particular China. In other words, de-industrialization is not happening everywhere; China is simply gaining a competitive edge and taking over manufacturing production from the rest of the world, becoming the world's factory.

Summary

We should not ignore or underestimate the growing ability of services to contribute to productivity growth, international trade, and, therefore, economic development at large. In this chapter, I showed, through various examples, how countries are benefiting from policies aimed especially at the growth of digital services. I highlighted the example of India, a country whose urban centres, including Bangalore and Hyderabad, are riding on the back of services-led growth in the ICT sector. At the same time, I cautioned against excessive hype about services-led development strategies, especially when it happens at the expense of the manufacturing sector. I gave three reasons for this.

First, the manufacturing sector still remains the backbone of productivity growth. If we take a closer look at the really productive services (mainly digital ones), they are highly dependent on manufactured products, including hardware chips, information transmission technologies, fibre optics, and satellites, to name a few. The same goes for other important services, such as delivery services, which, in addition to being dependent on the abovementioned technologies, also rely on transport equipment and mechanized warehouses. The manufacturing sector is at the core of technological progress, which is why firms associated with industrial production still employ a majority of scientists and engineers. Evidence shows us that very few countries have achieved an economic transformation from low to high income without a focus on manufacturing-led growth. The exceptions are mostly small countries that specialize in niche services, such as tourism and tax fraud, or obtain their wealth from highly valuable natural resources like oil.

Second, services can increasingly be traded across borders, but non-tradability still characterizes many services. On the other hand, all manufactured products can be traded. I did, however, mention that a new experimental data set suggests that services make up a much larger part of international trade than previously thought. I was specifically talking about GATS mode 3; the establishment of a commercial presence in another country. But calculations of trade in services through the inclusion of GATS mode 3 raises more questions than it answers, making a case against using GATS mode 3 in calculations on service trade. So, while we can certainly conclude that trade in services has increased in recent years, the exact amount is difficult to estimate. What we can say with certainty, though, is that large economies specializing in services at the expense of the manufacturing sector do face serious trade balance constraints. India and the United Kingdom are two good examples.

Third, measurement issues put into question the evidence behind the claim that the world economy has experienced a decline in manufacturing output. Many studies that scrutinize how we disaggregate economic activities in the national accounts argue that services that rely on engineering know-how and other production-related services should be classified as manufacturing in our national accounts, not as services. This goes especially for services that have come to add a significant share of economic value in global production networks, such as scientific and technical services (like R&D, industrial design, and testing), administrative and support services tailored for the manufacturing sector, and wholesale and retail trade services that are part and parcel of production systems. While it could, and should, be debated which of these services should be counted as manufacturing in countries' national accounts, research on this topic has made it clear that many services are closely intertwined with the manufacturing process, both geographically and through shared capabilities.

Even if we accept that manufacturing is counted 'correctly' in countries' national accounts, there is still good reason to question the claim that the world economy has experienced massive de-industrialization. If we look more closely at the data on global manufacturing, we will see that a lot of manufacturing has simply relocated to a small number of countries in East Asia, particularly China, rather than diminished everywhere.

To conclude, we should not dismiss the power of manufacturing to drive economic development and innovation. Yes, sources of economic prosperity are constantly changing, and especially digital services are helping some countries in the global South to catch up with countries in the global North. But factories still have an important role in shaping the world economy. In short, making things still matters.

3

Digital automation technologies

In 1811 in Arnold, Nottingham, a secret oath-based organization called the Luddites was established. The organization—consisting of textile artisans and weavers who had spent years learning the intricate craft of textile production using tools and hand-powered machinery—was formed to mobilize against the rise of factories that used automation technology in textile production. The backdrop for this was the Industrial Revolution, when technological advances in textile production resulted in the establishment and spread of big factories using steam-powered machinery that could automate tasks previously performed by humans. Some of the would-be Luddites tried to find jobs in the factories, but there simply weren't enough jobs: the machines had stolen most of them.

The Luddites' form of protest was not peaceful. They would normally meet at night on the moors surrounding industrial towns, breaking into factories to destroy machinery, burn down factories, and sometimes even exchange gunfire with company guards or soldiers. The Luddites hoped that their raids would deter factory owners from installing job-displacing machines, but instead, the British government made machine-breaking in textile factories punishable by death. Dozens of Luddites were either hanged or sent to Australia (where Great Britain sent many of its convicts throughout the nineteenth century). By 1813, the Luddite movement had more or less vanished due to the brutal measures enforced by the British government.

The first Industrial Revolution was a tough period not only for textile artisans but also for all wage labourers. For decades during the first Industrial Revolution, average real wages in Great Britain stagnated even as productivity rose.[1] Clearly, the introduction of new

The Future of the Factory. Jostein Hauge, Oxford University Press. © Jostein Hauge (2023).
DOI: 10.1093/oso/9780198861584.003.0004

technology, especially automation technology, can, and often does, displace labour. This is partly why the reputation of the Luddites has lived on. Today, the term 'Luddite' is used to describe someone opposed to automation, computerization, and the use of new technology. However, the hypothesis of many of today's Luddites—that automation will result in large-scale job displacement—has not played out. In the decades and centuries since the Industrial Revolution, automation technology has created a range of new jobs and unleashed demand for existing ones, more than offsetting the number of jobs it has destroyed. For example, a recent study by the global consultancy firm, McKinsey, calculated that the personal computer (PC) created 15.8 million more jobs than it displaced in the United States between 1980 and 2015.[2]

But there are rumblings that things are going to be different this time around, especially because of advances in artificial intelligence (AI). Only a few years ago, computer-based automation was limited by the need to be able to describe/codify every operation that needed to be done (also known as step-by-step instructions). This made it difficult for automation to be used in jobs involving abstract thinking, manual adaptability, and/or situational awareness, including high-skilled jobs such as creative design and low-skilled jobs like housework.[3] Today, new methods in machine learning, a subfield of AI, can enable digital systems to independently learn and apply rules. It is believed that this, combined with other technologies associated with the so-called fourth Industrial Revolution (including the miniaturization of computers, increased computing power, and continuous data collection through the internet-of-things) will make it easier to automate work across a range of industries in a short time frame.[4]

In fact, a growing body of work suggests that automation technologies will start displacing jobs at a faster rate than they have in the past.[5] In light of what this book is about, the roll-out of new, digital automation technologies warrants special attention because many studies suggest that jobs in the global South are at higher risk of automation,[6] especially routine jobs in the manufacturing sector or the job-creating potential of the manufacturing sector.[7] In this

chapter, I analyse the evidence on automation's impact on employment, job displacement, and reorganization of the labour force. First,
I look at the impact of automation on these variables in the past and
present. Then, I turn to the future, discussing so-called forecast studies. I also address the role of automation technologies in aiding and
accelerating reshoring and regionalization of supply chains.

Automation and employment in the distant and recent past

We all have a tendency to put disproportionate weight on the importance of current events, losing sight of how insignificant these events
often are when we place them in the context of history. The current
hype around automation technology is a good example. It's almost
as if today's rapid developments in AI are making people believe
that automation technology is something we, as a society, haven't
faced before. Of course, this is not true, as illustrated through my
example of the Luddite movement in the introduction to the chapter.
Automation technology used in industrial processes can actually be
traced back further than the Luddite movement: the first completely
automated machine was a flour mill developed in 1785 by Oliver
Evans.[8]

This means that the time frame available to assess the impact
of automation on employment and job displacement is long. The
Industrial Revolution is a good place to start as it's considered to
have been highly disruptive for workers. Technological advances
have never before enabled such a rapid and massive reorganization of the workforce from agriculture to manufacturing. The word
'reorganization' is important and should not be confused with job
displacement or unemployment. In fact, in many instances, automation technology during the Industrial Revolution created more jobs
than it displaced. In the nineteenth century US textile industry, 98%
of the labour required to weave cloth was automated. But because
jobs only got partially automated (e.g. by inventions that helped
workers replace empty bobbins or fix thread breaks), it reduced the

time it took a weaver to perform a task or reduced the frequency with which a task had to be performed. This increased labour productivity, driving the price of cloth down. In turn, this resulted in higher demand for cloth and hence employment growth in the textile industry.[9] Traditional textile artisans operating outside the factories, like the Luddites in Great Britain, might have been angry, but the textile industry as a whole saw employment growth over time.

However, reorganization of the workforce is still painful for a lot of workers. This was not only the case for the Luddites in the early nineteenth century but also for many agricultural workers throughout the nineteenth and twentieth centuries in most of today's high-income countries. As these countries industrialized, put heavier efforts into developing their manufacturing industries, and started to mechanize agriculture, demand for labour in the agricultural sector sharply declined. For example, in the United States, agriculture's share of total employment in the country dropped from 60% in 1850 to less than 5% by 1970. In countries that industrialized at a later stage, the shift from agriculture to industry has generally been more rapid. In China, one-third of its workforce moved (or was forced) out of agriculture between 1990 and 2015.[10] About the same time as China went through its period of early industrialization, many high-income countries went through a period of de-industrialization, which has also resulted in labour force restructuring that was painful for workers. In the United States, the manufacturing sector's share of total employment fell from 26% in 1960 to less than 10% in 2015, which is roughly the number today.[11] Detroit, once the heartland of US automotive manufacturing and popularly known as 'Motor City', suffered severely from de-industrialization and went through major economic decline in parallel to de-industrialization. The population of the city fell from 1,850,000 in 1950 to 680,000 in 2015. In 2013, Detroit filed the largest municipal bankruptcy case in US history. In recent years, the city's economy has started to grow again, but it wasn't many years ago that rumour had it you could buy a house in Detroit for less than $5,000.

We can already draw an important conclusion based on the analysis so far: since the first Industrial Revolution, we have continuously witnessed disruptions to, and reorganizations of, the labour force. However, automation is only partly to blame here. Another important variable is international competition. Especially after 1980, offshoring of production to the global South and increased international competition explains more job losses in the manufacturing sector in high-income countries than automation does.[12] Moreover, we should not discount how some people have lost their jobs or how some occupations have disappeared due to changes in demand (e.g. boarding housekeepers) or because of technological obsolescence (e.g. telegraph operators). Among the 271 occupations used in the 1950 US census, many have been partially automated or have disappeared altogether, but in only one case can the disappearance of an occupation be explained by automation: elevator operators.[13]

Let us move on to more recent use of automation technology, on which far more studies have been carried out, especially because of the growing interest in AI and related digital technologies. In high-income countries, the evidence of the impact of automation on employment is mixed. Some studies find that automation has displaced jobs,[14] but other studies emphasize different factors to explain job losses such as increased international competition;[15] a slowdown in productivity growth; [16] or demographic factors, for instance, a peak in women's participation in the labour force.[17] In the manufacturing sector specifically, studies more strongly conclude that automation technology in the recent past has displaced jobs.[18] However, one of these studies points out that job losses in manufacturing were fully offset by job growth in services.[19] Another one of these studies finds that not only has the loss of manufacturing been offset by more service jobs, but also net employment has actually been growing due to job growth in the service sector.[20]

We also need to keep in mind that job losses in the manufacturing sector in high-income countries in recent years is consistent with a trend of de-industrialization in these countries since the 1970s and has not accelerated since the introduction of new, digital automation technologies. This gives us reason to believe that other factors, such as the shift to services, offshoring of manufacturing to the global South, and increased international competition—factors that many of the abovementioned studies highlight—are equally, if not more, important in explaining the decline in manufacturing employment in high-income countries. One study actually finds that the adoption of automation technology in manufacturing increases employment within the sector. Using a panel data set of manufacturing firms in Spain between 1990 and 2016, the study finds that firms that had used robots in production generated jobs because output gains outweighed the reduction in labour intensity.

Workers in high-income countries make up only a small fraction of the global labour force. It is therefore important that we also look at the evidence of the impact of automation on job displacement with a global outlook in mind. The UN Industrial Development Organization has calculated that the annual growth in the stock of robots had a positive, albeit small, effect on global employment growth from 2000 to 2014, mostly within the manufacturing sector.[21] Looking specifically at the global South, the literature on automation is scarce. However, in the case of developing countries in Asia, the Asian Development Bank has provided some recent figures. It finds that new technologies (not specifically automation technologies) had a net positive impact on employment in 2005–2015, displacing 101 million jobs but creating 134 million jobs.[22] Similarly, a study on Latin America found that manufacturing firms in the region that invested in information and communications technology (ICT)—again, not automation technologies specifically—experienced net job gains.[23] In a recent study of the South African apparel industry, Christian Parschau and I have found that most firms that have adopted new automation technologies have increased levels of employment, largely due to the positive effect these technologies have had on productivity growth within the firms that adopted the technologies.

Generally, reports from international organizations note that most AI-related automation technologies are developed and used in the global North and have yet to make their inroad on a large scale in the global South.[24] An important reason for this is the many barriers that exist to implementing digital automation technologies in the global South. A report by the UN Conference for Trade and Development states that, 'Most existing studies overestimate the potential adverse employment and income effects of robots, because they neglect to take into account that what is technically feasible is not always also economically profitable.' [25] The report identifies many industries where this is the case, that is, industries that display automation potential from a technical standpoint but not from an economic standpoint. The report highlights especially the textile industry and the food industry because automation technology cannot compete with the low cost of labour in those industries. A number of additional barriers to implementing automation technologies exist in the global South, including a lack of trained maintenance people, a lack of access to capital, and unreliable energy infrastructure.[26]

In summary, although we see that automation technology has caused labour displacement and workforce disruptions in the near and distant past, the net effect on employment has generally been positive. This is due to a number of related reasons: (i) technological advancement is associated with productivity growth, which, over time, is associated with job growth; (ii) new technologies give rise to new industries and new jobs; (iii) the use of automation technologies can drive down the price of consumer goods or give rise to a larger variety of consumer goods, pushing demand and job growth upwards.

We should, of course, not dismiss the disruptive impact that automation technologies can have on certain sectors of the economy, and policy has an important role to play in mitigating such disruptions. Back in the early 1800s, during the Luddite raids, the British government could have done a better job at designing education and training policies to facilitate occupational transitions; manage adjustment costs; and, more broadly, 'reskill' the labour force. Such policies are now actively pursued in countries that experience rapid technological change. These kinds of policies are important because even though the 'net' impact of automation on employment is minimal, some sectors and industries suffer disproportionately.

Will things look the same in the future though, now that AI-related technologies are up-and-coming? There is a lot of hype surrounding AI, but the global market for AI, worth US$4.1 billion in 2018, constitutes a very small fraction of the global market for information technology as a whole, worth roughly $US5 trillion in that year.[27] Surveys suggest that businesses are interested in AI, but only a few of them are actually rolling out products that use AI-related technologies.[28] In the global South, less than 5% of manufacturing firms use advanced digital production technologies, and in some countries, over 70% of manufacturing firms only use analogue production technologies.[29] This could mean that the hype surrounding AI is excessive. But it could also mean that in the future, things will be different. So, it's important that we take a look at studies that forecast the future impact of automation on employment.

Automation and employment in the future

The 'bread and butter' of the literature on automation's impact on jobs is forecast studies—studies that predict how things will unfold in the future. This should come as no surprise seeing as so many AI-related technologies have been developed but not yet fully commercialized. Forecast studies are also the ones that have garnered the most attention. For example, Carl Benedikt Frey's and Michael Osborne's paper, 'The Future of Employment: How Susceptible Are Jobs to Computerisation?',[30] has been cited more than 10,000 times according to Google Scholar. Part of the attention the study has received is a testimony to the pioneering work of the study. It is the first rigorous study estimating the probability of automation across hundreds of occupations (702 occupations, to be precise). Still, the number of citations the study has racked up is astonishing, especially considering that the paper was published quite recently (in 2017). Though the number of citations to this particular study is impressive, we shouldn't be surprised at the attention these studies generally receive. People have always been drawn towards information (and entertainment, too, for that matter), imagining a future dominated by robots and other automation technology. You can even find a ranking of the hundred greatest movie robots of all time.[31]

In Figure 3.1, I have collated key studies published to date on the likely impact of automation on job displacement. The first and most important aspect to note about these studies is that their estimates for job displacement vary widely. For example, the study by Frey and Osborne finds that 47% of workers in the United States are at high risk of losing their jobs to automation in the 2020s and 2030s. On the other hand, Melanie Arntz and co-authors find that only 9% of workers in the United States and in other Organisation for Economic Co-operation and Development (OECD) countries are at high risk of losing their jobs to automation.[32]

Why do we see such discrepancies in estimates, even among studies that look at the impact of automation in the same country, like the two studies I just mentioned? A lot of it boils down to methodology. Arntz and co-authors say explicitly that a motivation for their study was the faulty assumption made in other studies, like the one by Frey and Osborne, that whole occupations could disappear when only a certain task in that occupation can be automated. In reality, many jobs are reconfigured, rather than lost, due to certain tasks being

Arntz et al. (2016)	9% of jobs in the United States (and 6–12% of workers in all OECD countries) are at high risk of automation.
Frey and Osborne (2017)	47% of workers in the United States are at high risk of losing their jobs to automation/computerization over the next few decades.
Manyika et al. (2017a, 2017b)	60% of all occupations in the world contain at least 30% technically automatable activities. However, reskilling is more likely than large-scale unemployment. By 2030, 75–375 million workers in the world will need to switch occupational categories. This does not break with historical trends of workforce restructuring.
PwC (2017)	The share of jobs potentially at risk of automation by the early 2030s: 30% in the United Kingdom, 38% in the United States, 35% in Germany, and 21% in Japan. Because new automation technologies will create jobs, and because of practical barriers to the implementation of automation, the net impact on employment is unclear.
World Bank (2016)	From a technological standpoint, two-thirds of all jobs in developing countries are susceptible to automation, but unemployment effects are moderated by low wages and slow technology adoption.
World Economic Forum (2020)	By 2025, 85 million jobs may be displaced by a shift in the division of labour between humans and machines, while 97 million new roles may emerge that are more adapted to the new division of labour between humans, machines, and algorithms.

Figure 3.1 Summary of forecast studies on automation

Source: Author's adaptation and update based on Parschau and Hauge (2020).

automated. The study by Arntz and co-authors takes into account the variety of worker's tasks within occupations, more in line with how things actually play out in the economy. Automation in the textile and apparel industry is a good case in point. Some forecast studies predict that sewing machine operators will lose their jobs due to automation[33] but fail to take into account the complexity involved in handling fabric. Fabric is difficult to handle by robotic devices because it is flexible and distorts. The sewing process involves a number of complex tasks, including guiding the fabric through a machine process, which require the constant intervention by an operator. This is why sewing cannot yet be fully automated (although certain tasks within the process can) and explains why robotic systems in use are highly bespoke and still limited to a few simple processes.[34]

The binary assumption in the study by Frey and Osborne—that an occupation can either be automated or not—is just one of its shortcomings. Another important shortcoming is that the study doesn't take into account jobs created by the introduction of new technology, both directly and indirectly, or the fact that it is more realistic to talk about labour reorganization in the economy rather than job displacement. With reference to the past, this is something I have discussed already, showing that while the introduction of new technologies has disrupted labour markets, societies have found ways to reorganize their workforces, especially because new technology creates jobs in addition to displacing them.

It is therefore a welcome sight that some forecast studies take a more granular approach to tasks within occupations and look deeper into how automation will reorganize the labour force rather than just estimating the probability of automation in certain occupations. For example, a forecast study published by McKinsey in 2017 finds that although 60% of occupations worldwide contain at least 30% activities that are automatable, only 5% of occupations have more than 90% automatable work.[35] This kind of conclusion is a direct reflection of taking a task-based rather than an occupation-based approach. Building on this study, a related report led by the same group of researchers at McKinsey estimate that between 75 and 275 million workers (3–14% of the global workforce) will need to switch occupational categories by 2030. The report stresses that this kind of reorganization of the workforce does not break with historical trends of workforce reorganization.[36] This is a very important conclusion because it means that even with the onset of digital, AI-related automation technologies, workforce reorganization and job displacement are predicted to be in line with how it has played out in the past.

The studies by McKinsey are not the only ones that take a more optimistic view on the actual labour market impact of automation technologies. In its 'Future of Jobs Report 2020', the World Economic Forum estimates that 85 million jobs may be displaced by 2025 due to a shift in the division of labour between humans and machines, but 97 million new roles could emerge that are more adapted to this new, digital age.[37] The multinational accounting firm, Price Waterhouse Coopers (PwC), reconciled methodologies from the studies by Frey and Osborne and Arntz and co-authors, and concluded that 20–40% of jobs could be at high risk of automation by the 2030s in Germany, Japan, the United Kingdom, and the United States.[38] But like the World Economic Forum, PwC cautions against extrapolating from automation to job displacement because the new technologies will create jobs and because of practical barriers to the implementation of automation. Similarly, the World Bank's World Development Report in 2016, thematically focusing on the role of digital technology in development, suggests that two-thirds of all jobs in developing countries are susceptible to automation but that unemployment effects will be moderated by low labour costs and slow technology adoption.[39]

It is clear that many forecast studies take an optimistic view—or at minimum, avoids a pessimistic view—on the impact of automation on overall employment. Thus, things might play out like they have in the past: automation could result in a reorganization of the labour force rather than causing large-scale unemployment. There are a few additional points about the forecast studies of which we should take note. The first is that we should be careful with making conclusions about the global South based on these studies because none of the rigorous studies actually use much data from the global

South. The study by McKinsey uses mostly labour market data from the United States to construct a global model. And the report by the World Bank, which does concern itself with the global South, only looks at this topic in the scope of a much bigger theme and hence does not apply the same methodological rigour as, for example, the studies by McKinsey, Frey and Osborne, and Arntz and co-authors. Second, the studies are projections going forward. The future is fundamentally uncertain so we should, by default, be sceptical of the estimates presented in these studies.

Moreover, many of the studies make a limited effort to properly analyse and discuss the potential barriers to implementing automation technologies—technological, economic, or geographical—or the expected time frame for the roll-out of these technologies. The study by McKinsey is the most detailed one, predicting early and late scenarios for automation of human work based on technical feasibility, financial feasibility, and regulatory/social barriers. The early scenario for automation of more than 50% of human work is 2035, while the late scenario is 2065. Carrying out such analyses is important because technology is a highly dynamic space where trajectories are tricky to predict. If my analysis earlier in this chapter is any indication, the pace of commercialization and the global spread of digital automation technologies in the future will look more like a marathon than a sprint.

Will automation technologies accelerate reshoring?

Considering the many barriers that exist to scaling up automation technologies especially in the global South, we may not see these technologies displace jobs directly in developing countries. However, they may do so indirectly through reshoring. Reshoring is essentially the reversal of offshoring: 'a reconcentration of parts of production from foreign locations as well as from foreign suppliers to the domestic production site of the company'.[40] Offshoring of production has been going on for decades now as lower trade and investment barriers have enabled high-income countries to cut costs by relocating production to countries that can offer cheaper labour. There is now a possibility that the implementation of digital automation technologies could reduce labour costs to the point that reshoring becomes economically feasible for transnational corporations—especially those based in the global North that, over the years, have offshored labour-intensive operations to the global South.[41]

In discussions on reshoring, a 'speedfactory' initiative by Adidas (the shoe and sports accessories manufacturer) launched in 2016 has received a lot of attention. The idea of the company's speedfactories was to manufacture shoes more or less from scratch in just a few hours with the help of highly advanced automation technology, employing almost no human labour. This would involve scaling down Adidas' labour-intensive shoe manufacturing in Asia, where the company has built up a sophisticated supply chain over many years. Adidas' first speedfactory was opened in Ansbach, Germany, in 2016, and a second speedfactory was opened near Atlanta, United States, in 2017. However, the factories were less successful than planned. In late 2019, Adidas announced that it would cease production at the speedfactories because they were unable to produce the high variety of models initially planned. An Adidas spokesperson also said that the know-how of existing Adidas suppliers in Asia turned out to be more important than anticipated. At present, Adidas still offshores most of its manufacturing to various suppliers in Asia. This is also the case for other large multinational shoe and textile manufacturers, such as Nike.[42]

Adidas is just one case though. What does the aggregate evidence tell us about reshoring trends? Reshoring is a relatively recent phenomena, but some large-scale studies have already been carried out which can help us to get a better idea of the big picture. These studies generally converge towards the conclusion that reshoring is rare. For example, a study by Bernhard Dachs and co-authors found that among 1,700 manufacturing firms in Austria, Germany, and Switzerland, only 4% had reshored activities in 2013 and 2014.[43] A similar study surveying 2,500 manufacturing firms in eight

European countries in 2015 found that less than 6% of surveyed firms had reshored activities in 2013–2015, while nearly 17% of firms had offshored activities over the same period.[44] This last point is important because although reshoring may occur or even accelerate, the job-displacement impact in the global South is negligible if offshoring occurs at a faster pace. We should also keep in mind that to the extent that reshoring happens, many factors are equally, if not more, important than cost-saving automation technology, including the added flexibility and security of leaner supply chains, improved quality control, unemployed capacity at home, the fear of intellectual property theft, and reduced transportation and coordination costs.[45]

These other factors are important to study because a more urgent need for reshoring due to, for example, a desire for leaner supply chains, could accelerate the scale-up of automation technologies. In fact, the COVID-19 pandemic and Russia's invasion of Ukraine has put reshoring at the centre stage of the agenda because it has exposed the fragility of global supply chains. It is also important to understand reshoring trends in the wake of these events, seeing that the abovementioned studies on reshoring were carried out before the events occurred. How are these events exactly related to reshoring though? In short, the COVID-19 pandemic and Russia's invasion of Ukraine has rattled the global economy, causing huge swings in both global supply/demand patterns and prices of globally traded commodities. Given the existence of globally fragmented and complex supply chains for more or less all goods, production processes have become more fragile: that is, the resilience of the entire chain is only as strong as the weakest link of the chain. The pandemic and the war in Ukraine exposed the fragility of this global interconnectedness, and now we have huge backlogs and delays in several parts of many different supply chains. (In Chapter 5, I discuss the pandemic's impact on globalized production in greater detail.) The way that these events have exposed this fragility has made many firms and countries more aware of the vulnerability of being dependent on imports of inputs and commodities from far-away places. Hence, many firms and countries are saying that they need to reshore (or nearshore or regionalize) their supply chains at a faster pace.

In theory, the consequences of this sound scary, but in practice, is COVID-19 induced reshoring happening? The short answer is: barely. The long answer is a bit more complicated. Global supply chains are complex structures that have been built up over many years, and industrial know-how, capabilities, and tacit knowledge has been developed in specific geographical locales based on specialization patterns. While the chains are fragile (the pandemic clearly proved this), it is not straightforward to remould or rebuild the chains. Adidas' reshoring attempt is a perfect example as it demonstrated how important their Asian supply chain was, not only for cheap labour but also for the technological capabilities and innovation systems developed there. While it is fair to expect that reshoring will ramp up due to the pandemic, it is very important to pay attention to the scale of reshoring.

News headlines might give the impression that the pandemic has spelled the death knell for global supply chains. This couldn't be further from the truth. An article published in the *Financial Times* in May 2022 is a great example of how reading the fine print on reshoring articles matters a lot.[46] The headline reads: 'UK Manufacturers "Reshore" Supply Chains after Pandemic and Brexit'. The article cites a survey carried out by Make UK, the largest manufacturers trade group in the United Kingdom.[47] The survey is therefore a great indication of intents to reshore in one of the countries that has seen its supply chains rattled the most because of the double whammy of Brexit and the pandemic. The survey reveals that 75% of UK-based companies have increased their supply from other UK-based companies since 2020. In other words, reshoring has clearly accelerated. But the survey also reveals that only 10% of UK-based companies are planning to reduce reliance on Asian suppliers over the next two years. More interestingly, the survey shows that more companies are planning to increase than decrease supply from distant locations. From this we can deduce that (i) reshoring is accelerating on a *small scale* and (ii) offshoring will likely continue to outpace reshoring. Figures on global goods trade support this conclusion. A World Trade Organization (WTO) press release from October 2021 showed that global trade in goods had already surpassed pre-pandemic levels by the end of the second quarter in 2021.[48] A later WTO press release, from October 2022, showed steady growth of global trade in goods, even when accounting for the impact of the war in Ukraine.[49] While global trade in goods is not a perfect proxy for trade in supply chains, this evidence is sufficient to conclude that reshoring on a large scale has not happened since the onset of the pandemic or Russia's invasion of Ukraine. And the survey by Make UK indicates that large-scale reshoring is unlikely to happen in the near future.

Summary

Digital automation technologies have the potential to disrupt jobs, industries, and entire economies. In this chapter, I investigated the impact of automation technologies on employment and job displacement in the past, present, and future, focusing on the manufacturing sector. The takeaway message: evidence suggests that automation technologies will result in a reorganization of the labour force rather than large-scale job displacement and unemployment, in line with historical trends. Sectors will be impacted differently, and labour-intensive manufacturing is one sector that apparently stands out to lose more jobs. But even in this sector, studies find that the net impact of automation on employment thus far is negligible or even positive. In this sense, industrialization as a development strategy is not under significant threat.

Automation technologies create, as well as destroy, jobs through many channels: (i) technological advancement is associated with productivity growth, which, in the long run, is associated with job growth; (ii) new technologies give rise to new industries and new jobs; (iii) the use of automation technologies can drive down the price of consumer goods or give rise to a larger variety of consumer goods, pushing demand and job growth upwards. This is why the

PC has created so many more jobs than it has displaced. Of course, we should not dismiss the disruptive impact that automation technologies can have on certain sectors of the economy. Textile artisans in the 1800s (the Luddites) raided and destroyed textile factories for a reason. Workers in America's rustbelt have not just lost their jobs due to international competition; automation technology has definitely played a role. Therefore, we need to have strategies in place to mitigate the negative impact of automation on labour markets. Luckily, we have become better at it. Unlike the British government in the early 1800s, most governments today have education and training policies in place to facilitate occupational transitions; manage adjustment costs; and, more broadly, 'reskill' the labour force.

However, with advances in AI, will things look the same way in the future? There is a lot of hype surrounding AI, but the global market for AI is still just a small fraction of the entire market for ICT. In the global South, not many manufacturing firms use advanced digital production technologies. The hype around AI seems excessive. But the slow roll-out of AI-related technologies could also imply that we have just touched the tip of the iceberg of AI and that future scenarios will break with historical trends of job displacement and labour market reorganization. Forecast studies on automation seem to caution against such narratives though. The most detailed forecast studies arrive at similar conclusions, which is that automation technologies will likely lead to more jobs gained than jobs lost. Some of the forecast studies also provide modest job-displacement estimates because they recognize that automation technologies often only displace tasks within an occupation rather than the entire occupation.

Most of the detailed studies on automation's impact on job displacement use data from Europe and North America, so we need to be careful with extrapolating and drawing conclusions for the global South based on these studies. The studies that do focus on the global South highlight that the implementation of digital automation technologies will likely be much slower there than in the global North due to a number of additional barriers, such as lack of access to capital, unreliable energy infrastructure, and lack of trained maintenance people. The UN Conference for Trade and Development argues that existing studies with a global view overestimate the adverse employment effects of automation because they forget to take into account that technical feasibility does not translate into economic feasibility.

There is, however, a concern that jobs in the global South will not be lost due to automation technologies directly implemented there but rather lost through reshoring efforts in the global North (aided by automation technologies). But studies on reshoring find that reshoring is happening on a small scale and continues to be outpaced by offshoring. Even with the global supply chain chaos caused by the COVID-19 pandemic and Russia's invasion of Ukraine, manufacturing companies in high-income countries are not planning to massively ramp up reshoring. While it is expected that reshoring will accelerate, global supply chains are complex structures that are not easy to take apart and remould. Adidas' failed reshoring attempt is a perfect example as it demonstrated how important its Asian supply chain was, not only for cheap labour but also for the technological capabilities and innovation systems developed there.

4
Globalization of production

Industrialization and globalization are closely connected. For centuries, countries that have had strong industrial sectors have also had a strong presence in international trade networks. Seeing that all manufactured products can be traded across borders, it makes complete sense for countries that make such products to utilize opportunities for trade to reach new markets, to achieve the benefits of ramping up production (economies of scale), and to generate export earnings.

Globalization is not a recent phenomenon. It's not easy to say exactly when it 'started'—some people say that complex cross-border trade networks can be traced back to 6500 BC around the Tigris–Euphrates river system. Over the centuries, we have witnessed many waves of globalization, but the movement of goods and capital across borders started picking up notable pace with the onset of the Industrial Revolution and capitalist production. The First and Second World Wars put some dents in the pace of globalization, but since about 1980 we have been living in an age of hyper-globalization. This is evidenced by several trade metrics, including an explosive growth in global exports and imports, foreign direct investment, and intermediate goods trade.[1] Globalization in the past few decades is the result of many factors, including lowered trade barriers, the spread of neoliberalism, reduced transport costs, and rapid advances in information and communication technology. In particular, cheaper and more reliable telecommunications, information management software, and increasingly powerful computers have decreased the costs of organizing and coordinating complex economic activities over long distances.[2]

The Future of the Factory. Jostein Hauge, Oxford University Press. © Jostein Hauge (2023).
DOI: 10.1093/oso/9780198861584.003.0005

A fascinating part of the era of globalization we are living in now is how production systems have become. and are becoming, increasingly fragmented and how tasks and activities within these production systems have dispersed globally. This has led to complex and borderless business networks and production systems, popularly referred to as global value chains, global production networks, and/or global supply chains.[3] The iPhone is a perfect example. I outlined this example in detail in the introductory chapter of this book, showing how, although Apple designs and sells the iPhone as its product, the company actually doesn't manufacture any of the phone's components. Instead, Apple outsources the actual production and assembly of the phone's many components to a range of companies and countries, mostly in Asia. Complex value chains like these are not unique to the iPhone. More or less all the 'stuff' that is consumed today—from cars, bicycles, and computers to furniture, toys, and clothes—moves through a global value chain before it is sold to the final consumer.

We clearly see that, today, specializing in the production of a good and trading that good is not the same as in the old days. In the early 1800s, the famous economist, David Ricardo, used the example of wine and cloth to describe how countries would specialize in the production of different goods and benefit from trading these goods with each other. Today, countries specialize in different activities within both wine and cloth value chains. For example, in a cloth value chain (or rather, apparel value chain, which is a term more commonly used today), some firms, and even entire countries, specialize in just cutting, sewing, and trimming textile that is imported from other countries. In turn, the firms and countries specializing in textile production often import the raw material (cotton) from firms in yet another set of countries.

While specialization patterns are different today compared to Ricardo's time, his example still has a profound influence on how people theorize the benefits of international trade. Ricardo showed how, if each country specializes in producing and trading the good with the relatively lowest cost of production, that good in which the country has a 'comparative advantage' in producing and trading, the entire world benefits.[4] Most people agree that Ricardo's theory is not a perfect representation of the world, but his theory of comparative advantage remains an important justification for the benefits of international trade and globalization. This has also become the case for global value chains: a growing literature highlights that participation in global value chains is often positively correlated with industrialization, economic development, and growth and that countries can utilize global value chains to develop competitive industrial capabilities through pathways that weren't available to them only a few decades ago.[5]

In this chapter, I critically investigate the idea that global value chains are beneficial to industrialization and economic development. Drawing on old and new wisdom, I will show how participation in global value chains is not a panacea for development, especially for countries in the global South. In particular, I will show how the benefits of participating in global value chains are highly unequal, most often favouring transnational corporations based in the global North. I will also look at how international trade agreements impact the policy space developing countries have to implement policies important to develop and upgrade within global value chains. In the final section of the chapter, I will discuss how the COVID-19 pandemic has impacted global production and what it means for industrialization pathways.

How the globalization of production is beneficial for economic development

The expansion of global value chains has important implications for economic development and industrialization as it is enabling countries in the global South to participate in the global economy on an unprecedented scale. In the years since the 1980s, countries in the global South have considerably increased their share of global trade (see Figure 4.1). Given this opportunity for countries in the global

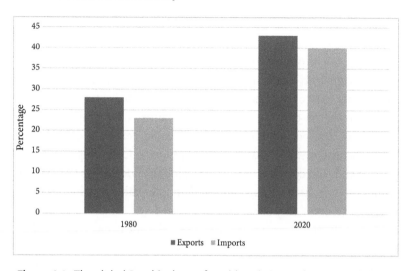

Figure 4.1 The global South's share of world trade in goods, 1980 and 2020

Note: United Nations Conference on Trade and Development (UNCTAD) Data Center uses the term 'developing economies', which is used as a proxy for the global South in this figure.
Source: Author, based on data from UNCTAD Data Center.

South to participate in global production systems on a larger scale, industrialization and industrial policy in the context of global value chains is drawing more interest.[6]

From the perspective of countries in the global South, participating in global value chains can have many benefits for economic development and industrialization. In the short term, it can boost employment, increase export and tax revenues, assist integration into the world economy, and have a positive impact on infrastructure development. In the long term, participation in global value chains can assist the transfer of technology and knowledge from transnational corporations to firms and workers in the country operations are offshored to, that is, the 'host' country.[7] This is particularly true when participation in global value chains from the perspective of a developing country entails the attraction of foreign direct investment, which it often does. Especially in the time since the Second World War, rapid economic development, industrialization, and technological catch-up has not been a process of innovation as much as a process of imitation—a process of acquiring technologies that more developed countries already have, often embedded in the practices of transnational corporations, frequently generated through their corporate research and development (R&D). The so-called 'Asian tigers'[8] are the best examples as they achieved rapid industrialization and technological catch-up through strategically participating in international trade networks.[9] In fact, over the past few decades, the United States has lost many high-tech industrial capabilities to competitor countries in East Asia and is now scrambling to bring many of these capabilities back.[10]

Another positive development is that, in the age of global value chains, countries can join value chains and supply chains rather than build them from scratch.[11] As I mentioned, the Asian tigers strategically participated in international trade networks and, to some extent, global value chains. However, since the rapid industrialization of the Asian tigers, production has become increasingly fragmented globally, and it has become easier for developing countries to join segments of value chains. Richard Baldwin, an economist and expert on international trade, says, 'Before 1985, successful industrialization meant building a domestic supply chain. Today, industrialisers join supply chains and grow rapidly because offshored production brings elements that took Korea and Taiwan decades to develop domestically.' [12] In other words, global value chains are making it relatively easier for countries in the global South to develop niche industrial capabilities because these countries now have the opportunity to specialize in particular segments of an industry (stages of production, tasks, or business functions) without having all the 'upstream' capabilities in place. This means that developing countries can start exporting sophisticated products more quickly at a lower cost.

From the perspective of developing countries, the participation in global value chains often happens through the construction of special economic zones, which are also sometimes referred to as industrial parks or export processing zones. A special economic zone is a geographically enclosed zone (secured, for example, by a fence or a wall) that often provides special financial incentives and favours for foreign firms (although, in some instances, for domestic firms).

Normally, the idea behind the construction of a special economic zone is to produce goods for the purpose of exports. The financial incentives are put in place by the host country to more easily attract foreign investment, making it financially lucrative for foreign firms to set up production facilities in the special economic zone. Alongside the expansion of global value chains, the number of special economic zones in the world has skyrocketed. This number stood at 79 in 1975, 500 in 1995, and 5,400 in 2019.[13] China represents roughly 50% of this increase, and the country is one of the best examples of reaping the benefits of participating in global value chains. In addition to the establishment of special economic zones, another key measure of a country's participation in global value chains is how much that country exports processed goods, goods that use imported inputs. Between 2000 and 2008, a time when China's economic growth rate was at peak levels, the country accounted for 67% of the world's exports in processed goods.[14] Given the fast growth of participation in global value chains during China's rapid economic development period, it is undeniable that global value chains can have a positive impact on economic development and industrialization in the global South.

How the globalization of production hinders economic development

The opportunities for economic development accompanied by participation in global value chains are closely linked: the manufacturing and production activities brought about by foreign investments are normally tied to a segment of a global value chain, often in the context of a special economic zone. But although the expansion of global value chains is surely accompanied by opportunities for economic development and industrialization, the dark side of this expansion, at times ignored in publications by the mainstream international development community,[15] needs to be highlighted.

The story of trade liberalization in Mexico

In those cases where participation in global value chains does not yield benefits, it is often due to the lack of technological spillovers from foreign firms to the host country or the lack of linkages from foreign firms to the host countries. In fact, econometric studies trying to find a relationship between the attraction of foreign investment and productivity growth in the host country are, at best, ambiguous.[16] Export processing zones do tend to increase exports in the host country, but a high share of domestic content in exports is the exception rather than the rule. In most cases, less than 10% of inputs used for exports in export-processing zones are purchased domestically.[17]

Mexico's period of trade liberalization, starting in the 1980s, is a prime example of how the attraction of foreign investment and participation in global value chains can go wrong. Prior to liberalization (1950s–1980s), Mexico was known for its strict stance towards foreign investors. For example, in the information and communication technology (ICT) sector, a sector that was hugely important for Mexico, transnational corporations were limited to 49% equity ownership in joint ventures with domestic firms; they had to invest between 3 and 6% of gross sales into domestic R&D; and domestic parts and components had to account for at least 45% of value added for personal computers (PCs).[18] By the early 1980s, some Mexican firms (for instance, Scale and Electron Computers) manufactured their own computers. Mexican assembly manufacturers working alongside transnational corporations were also starting to make a name for themselves, including Electronica Panter and Microtron, who, in some instances, supplied global firms like International Business Machines (IBM), Motorola, Hewlett Packard (HP), and Kodak.[19] By 1987, an impressive 56% of domestic demand in Mexico's ICT industry was met by domestic supply.[20]

This protectionist strategy was successful in generating growth and diversification of the domestic ICT sector, but it was not very successful in making domestic firms internationally competitive.

By the mid-1980s, continuing trade balance problems and a debt crisis (the plunge in the oil price in 1982 being an important factor) swung the pendulum towards neoliberalism. After signing the North American Free Trade Agreement (NAFTA) in the early 1990s, the shift towards free trade was more or less complete. The plan of Carlos Salinas, the new president (1988–94) who endorsed neoliberal policies, was to create jobs and modernize the economy through attracting foreign investment. Global flagships of the ICT industry at the time, like HP and IBM, moved massive manufacturing assembly operations to Guadalajara, Mexico as wages were low, labour unions weak, there was proximity to the US market, and tariffs were eventually lowered to zero under NAFTA.[21] In the early 2000s, more than 90% of foreign investment into developing countries was dispersed between only ten countries, and Mexico was in the top three.[22]

While transnational corporations flourished in Mexico, the domestic computer industry became almost extinct. There were initial hopes that local firms would evolve into contract manufacturers and suppliers to the US-based transnational corporations, but these hopes were short-lived. Companies like HP and IBM invited contract manufacturers based in the United States instead, such as Flextronics and Solectron, to co-locate in Guadalajara. In turn, these contract manufacturers built their competitive advantage by managing a third tier of local suppliers, mostly in East Asia. Less than 5% of inputs were sourced from Mexico.[23] Not only were transnational corporations who came to Mexico free to import all of their inputs, but there were no policies in place to ensure knowledge transfer. The skill content of jobs given to Mexican workers was extremely low, thus generating limited knowledge spillovers. Among the employees of foreign firms in Guadalajara, only 6.9% had graduated from high school. On top of this, transnational corporations carried out almost no R&D activities in Mexico. They saw the country primarily as a place for assembly operations. This, in part, explains why labour productivity in Mexico has steadily risen since the 1990s whereas real wages in Mexico have not.[24]

The attraction of firms from the United States was initially a source of employment and income, but this changed in the early

2000s. The dot-com stock bubble burst, making US-based firms search for cheaper production sites. China's World Trade Organization (WTO) membership in 2001 could not have come at a better time. China became the lead production platform for these firms, and manufacturing operations in Guadalajara were severely cut back or relocated.

So, who is to blame for this lack of technological spillovers? Kevin Gallagher and Lyuba Zarsky argue that the promise of Mexico's 'Silicon Valley' went unfulfilled for two reasons.

One is the global restructuring and increased competition of the ICT industry. The emergence of China as a key player in the global production system, with a rare combination of low wages, a huge domestic market, and impressive productive capabilities, made it more difficult for Mexico to compete internationally. The second is the lack of government policies aimed at building capabilities of local firms. From the mid-1980s onwards, Mexico's government failed to put in place incentives for foreign firms to use domestic inputs; there was no government-provided development financing for domestic firms; and high interest rates choked domestic investments and put upward pressure on the peso, which further biased procurement from transnational corporations away from domestic suppliers. As Gallagher and Zarsky write,

> The experience of other late-industrialising countries, especially in East Asia, is that the state must proactively promote local learning, knowledge, and innovation. With such policies in place, FDI [foreign direct investment] spillovers can be garnered. Without them and the growth of local knowledge assets they engender, MNCs [multinational corporations] will transfer only low-skilled, low-wage and ultimately footloose operations. Rather than a proactive industry policy to develop domestic firms and markets, Mexico adopted a 'maquila mindset' that oriented industrial development solely around attracting MNCs to produce for export.[25]

The fate of Mexico holds important lessons for how to (or not to) utilize global value chains for the purpose of economic development:

without an active state to 'guide' the market, economic development trajectories are subject to the whims of transnational corporations, who, in essence, answer only to the profit-seeking missions of their managers, owners, and shareholders. The fate of Mexico also shows us that the world economy has progressively become an arena where sovereign states compete against one another and that someone is always looking to outsmart or undercut you to gain a competitive edge. In this particular case, it was China that outsmarted and undercut Mexico.

The race to the bottom and the fallacy of composition

Competition has become especially fierce among countries in the global South. With greater participation of China and other Southeast Asian countries in the global economy, the global South's share of low-tech manufacturing exports has almost tripled since 1980 and the global pool of unskilled labour has doubled since 1990.[26] Former Chief Economist of the World Bank, Justin Lin, has argued that China's wages will eventually rise, giving a window of opportunity for lower-income countries, especially in Africa, to enter global manufacturing networks. However, low-wage labour capacity in the Asian production system is far from tapped. Countries like Bangladesh, Cambodia, India, and Vietnam have developed better capabilities to take over China's low-wage production than most African countries currently have. Alongside untapped capacity in Asia's production system, the number of people looking for work in Africa is rapidly increasing. Africa's population is growing at an astonishing rate: by 2030, the region is expected to have 1.6 billion people. With the current youth bulge in Africa (the median age is twenty years), it is estimated that 800 million people will be eligible for work in 2030 compared to 460 million in 2010.[27] The majority of the current working population in Africa end up in informal jobs, which means that a colossal number of jobs would have to relocate from Asia to Africa to absorb this surplus. So, if anything, the global competition in manufacturing will become even fiercer, with what seems like an endless supply of labour in Asia and Africa in the years to come.

The result is that transnational corporations based in the global North are likely to continue to enjoy a 'race to the bottom' among countries in the global South—declining global wages as a consequence of an abundant supply of unskilled labour and low labour standards in those countries. At the same time, countries in the global South are likely to suffer from a 'fallacy of composition'—they are all competing against one another in segments of global manufacturing with low-entry barriers. The result is that profit margins and export earnings are squeezed to the point that it doesn't translate into economic development.

The expanding power of transnational corporations

There is, however, more explaining to do behind the dark side of the expansion of global value chains. The story so far does not fully capture how power asymmetries favouring transnational corporations in the global North dictate development outcomes in the global South. Since the days of Mexico's maquila factories, the criticism of global value chains has steadily been mounting; a criticism emphasizing the oligopoly-driven structure of global value chains and asymmetric power relations within global value chains.[28] In essence, large and powerful transnational corporations—mostly headquartered in the global North—often use their growing dominance and power in the global economy to squeeze and minimize the profits of firms and wages of labour in the global South. In many ways, the rise of global value chains restates the relevance of the theories of uneven development that I discussed in Chapter 1, postulating that poor states are impoverished by the way they are integrated into the world system through a relationship of uneven economic exchange with wealthy states.

A snapshot of the geographical dispersion of the world's largest transnational corporations reveals a high concentration in the global

North, especially the United States.[29] This global dominance of transnational corporations based in the global North ('lead firms' in global value chain jargon) has been documented broadly: a handful of firms, mostly based in the global North, have accounted for 50% or more of the market share in more or less every global industry since about 2000,[30] and companies from the United States have the leading profit shares among the world's top 2,000 firms in a majority of sectors.[31] While power asymmetries in the world economy have always existed, it has worsened particularly since the late 1970s: the income collected by US-based transnational corporations from their foreign affiliates increased from 17% in 1977 to 49% in 2006, measured as a share of their total worldwide net income.[32] Transnational corporations are, in many instances, more important players in the world economy than powerful countries. For example, Wal-Mart, one of the world's largest retail companies, ranked as China's seventh largest trading partner in 2010, ahead of the United Kingdom.[33]

Given the global consolidation and expansion of transnational corporations based in the global North, it should come as no surprise to hear that these are the firms who walk away with the lion's share of profits in global manufacturing. But they are rarely the ones who actually make the products. The electronics industry, one of the world's largest consumer industries, is a good case in point. The world's largest exporter of electronics is China, but the country only accounts for 3% of global profits in the electronics industry. The United States, by comparison, accounts for 33% of global profits in the electronics industry, while not exporting nearly as many goods in this industry as China does.[34] Why is this? It can partly be explained by the global control and power that firms in the United States have amassed over the years. Among other things, this allows these powerful lead firms to push down prices of supplies and inputs to marginal cost and thus extract the full profits from the sales of the final goods, known as the 'mark-up effect'.[35] William Milberg and Deborah Winkler document how the price of manufactured goods imports into the United States have declined steadily relative to consumer prices in the Unites States between the 1980s and the 2000s, in some instances by more than 40%.[36]

Another explanation behind this uneven distribution of value and profits is the protection of intellectual property—protection most often arising from the filing and use of patents, copyrights, and trademarks. Knowledge monopolies and protection of intellectual property among powerful transnational corporations are driving intense concentration of corporate wealth and power, thereby holding back catch-up by countries in the global South.[37] A recent paper by Cedric Durand and William Milberg gets this point across forcefully. They find a humongous increase in international income generated by intellectual property rights from the 1980s to the 2010s, almost entirely going to high-income countries (dominated by the United States). In 1980, the income generated from international payments related to the use of intellectual property was fairly equal across the world. In 2016, this income was a hundred times higher in high-income countries than in low—and middle-income countries (US$323 billion versus US$3 billion).[38] Durand and Milberg don't mince their words in sharing their view on this development, stating clearly that transnational corporations based in high-income countries are increasing their profit shares in global value chains mainly thanks to stronger protection of intellectual property and that this development is complementary to the expansion of global value chains:

In sum, the stricter IP [intellectual property] regime initiated by the US in the early eighties spread rapidly across the world economy in the 1990s and 2000s while GVCs [global value chains] trade expanded. These two trends are complementary. The extension of legal intellectual monopoly mostly benefited firms based in high-income economies. The international distribution of IP-related payments shows the dominance of enterprises based in high-income countries, which is both the rationale for, and the result of, their efforts to broaden and tighten IPRs [intellectual property rights] during the past decades.[39]

The injustice arising from this international system of intellectual property protection is exacerbated by many bilateral, regional, and international trade agreements, including the agreement on

Trade-Related Aspects of Intellectual Property Rights (TRIPS) within the WTO. In practice, this agreement prevents the transfer of intellectual property and technology to the global South and will be discussed in greater detail later in this chapter.

The production of an iPhone is a telling example of the uneven distribution of value and profits in a global value chain. Let us revisit this particular value chain, which I broke down in the introduction, but now let's also look at the distribution of value among different actors. In Figure 4.2, I have calculated the average distribution of value for iPhones released between 2010 and 2018. The figure is nothing short of shocking. Throughout practically every new iPhone release, Apple has been raking in 56% of the final retail price (on average) without actually producing or assembling any of the components. Of the final retail price, 1.5% goes to the most labour-intensive part of the production stage—assembly, mostly carried out in China. In other words, the workers who actually make the

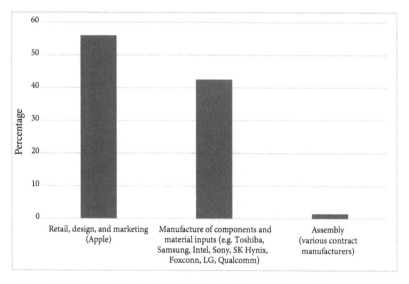

Figure 4.2 Average distribution of value for iPhones released between 2010 and 2018

Note: Specifically, three iPhones, including iPhone 4, iPhone 7, and iPhone X.
Source: Hauge (2021).

world's most popular phone pocket almost none of the profits from sales.

Labour standards and global poverty chains

According to the International Labour Organization, 30% of all workers in the world made less than US$150 per month in 2017, adjusted for purchasing power.[40] The adjustment for purchasing power makes this figure especially shocking—think of the entire world as the United States (with those living costs) and 30% of the world's population making less than US$150 per month. This is horrifying. If this was actually the case in the United States, people would be outraged. But because of the intricate and complicated global web of production systems today, consumers in the global North have little or no relationship to the workers in the global South that make their products. Many of us therefore don't bat an eyelid at statistics like these. The shockingly low wages at the bottom rung of the global labour force can, to some degree, be attributed directly to the globalization of production—real wages have declined the most in sectors that have been increasingly exposed to international competition, particularly the automotive sector, the apparel sector, the electronics sector, and other factory-related sectors.[41] The case of the iPhone that I detailed earlier is a telling example.

The race to the bottom in global labour standards is clearly part and parcel of unregulated globalization of production. Benjamin Selwyn, a scholar who investigates the role of labour in global production, states that 'the global manufacturing system has become a structure through which lead firms seek to enhance their global positions and strategies for extended capital accumulation and profit maximisation in relation to supplier firms, would-be competitor firms, and labouring classes'.[42] This is why Selwyn calls for global value chains to be relabelled 'global poverty chains'. The worker's perspective, which Selwyn emphasizes, should not be overlooked. The value squeeze I have outlined in this section is also a value squeeze on labour, which is part and parcel of the dire working conditions in factories and special economic zones across the global South, evidenced by wages below the social reproduction wage, excessive overtime work, and damaging health conditions.[43]

An investigation by Selwyn into footwear manufacturing in Cambodia and electronics manufacturing in China underscores the dreadful labour standards in global value chains. Across Cambodia's garment and footwear industry, almost 2,000 people fainted due to overly hot workplace conditions within the span of only one year (2015). In China's electronics sector, minimum wage increases have been commended, but these wage increases have been offset by cutting worker subsidies and making workers liable for workplace insurance. In terms of total monetary compensation, workers are often worse off.[44] Cambodia and China are often used as examples of countries that are successfully embracing globalization, but the investigations into working conditions in export-oriented factories and special economic zones in these two countries clearly tell a different story.

The race to the bottom in labour standards due to globalized production is not unique to the twenty-first century. During the industrialization of the Asian 'tigers', labour movements were often subdued in order to keep wages low and competitiveness high. Especially in South Korea, but also in Singapore, the state curtailed organized labour by repressing and co-opting independent unions. In Hong Kong and Taiwan, the intermingling of kinship ties and business networks limited the emergence of working-class militancy.[45]

Given that industrialization in the age of globalized production has often involved dreadful working conditions and a suppression of labour movements, both in the late twentieth and early twenty-first centuries, we need to come up with solutions to improve labour standards. There is hope, though, because low labour standards can impact industrialization negatively. In an investigation I carried out with Vincent Hardy into labour challenges in Ethiopia's apparel and footwear industries, we found that high turnover rates reduced competitiveness among export-oriented firms.[46] Investors and managers we interviewed were almost unanimous in describing turnover as the most common and costly issue. But why was turnover so high? The reason was simple: low wages, hazardous conditions, and little agency. The case of Berhanu, a twenty-six-year-old sewing operator, shows that when 'voice' fails, 'exit' is often the only alternative:

> Well, we worked standing all day and the machinery was heavy. And they don't consider that on your payment, there are no incentives or bonuses and besides there were chemicals. It affected our skins; they don't provide you with safety equipment. I quitted for such reasons. We asked our supervisors, I waited for them to get better day after day but they don't care so I left.

Many textile and leather manufacturing firms in Ethiopia responded by offering better benefits to workers, including subsidized lunches, health-care services, and annual leave. These developments did, however, occur alongside a curtailment of labour power in both its individual and collective forms. But this case study should give us hope because it shows that better working conditions are not antithetical to industrialization and international competitiveness.

In short, while the expansion of global value chains is accompanied by some opportunities for countries in the global South to integrate into the world economy in a beneficial manner, it also comes with massive challenges. In this section, I have showed how the expansion of global value chains has enabled a small number of large, transnational corporations—mostly based in the global North—to appropriate increasing shares of profits over a larger market. This appropriation is fortified by technological dominance, strong protection of intellectual property, low trade barriers, and privileged access to low-cost capital and labour all over the world. The uneven distribution of value and profits in twenty-first-century global value chains are often depicted by the deepening smile of the 'smile curve' (see Figure 4.3). This deepening (the arrows in the figure) is driven by the dynamics I have just outlined, all contributing to a more favourable global environment for transnational corporations mainly based in the global North. If you compare Figure 4.2 (the distribution of value for iPhones) and Figure 4.3 (the

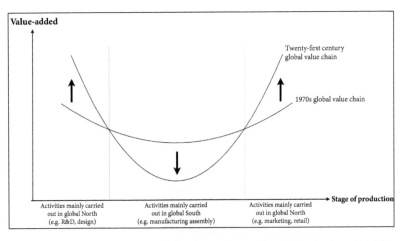

Figure 4.3 The smile curve and the deepening smile of global value chains
Source: Author, inspiration taken from various existing versions.

smile curve), you will see that they both convey this message. The difference is that the smile curve is a generalized version of this message.

The version of the smile curve I have created here does not illustrate all stages of production and is not always an accurate representation of how value is distributed in each and every global value chain. For example, the manufacture of many high-tech and low-tech components that go into making a final product often falls somewhere between the left and middle part of the smile and takes place in countries in both the global South and the global North. Nevertheless, the smile curve helps to illustrate some key takeaway messages from this section: the era of dominance by transnational corporations based in the global North has (i) made it harder for countries in the global South to break into higher-value added industries and stages of production in value chains, (ii) reduced the value and profits of many manufacturing activities that already take place in many countries in the global South, and (iii) contributed to dire working conditions and supressed wages in factories and special economic zones across the global South.

The globalization of production and international trade agreements

The globalization of production has changed the nature of industrialization. The international division of labour within sectors has become more pronounced (e.g. countries specialize in producing parts of a car, not the entire car) and countries in the global South have come to rely more on transnational corporations for their own industrialization. In the age of globalized production, certain policy instruments have therefore become more important for economic development. Some good examples of such policies would be those intended to avoid domestic firms, or even entire domestic economies, becoming trapped in low-value segments of global value chains and policies intended to transfer technology from foreign firms to the domestic economy. In a sense, policies intended to avoid the fate of the computer industry in Mexico have become more important in the age of globalized production.

Policies within this scope would normally be categorized as trade policies, and when there is talk about trade policies, things get messy. The reason for this is that trade policies creates both winners and losers in the global economy. One country's tariffs, export subsidies, or restrictions on foreign investment can hurt another country's ambitions to enter new markets with goods or capital. This is why trade wars happen: countries retaliate against one another through the use of trade policies, quite often by raising import tariffs. The solution to trade wars is trade agreements. Among all the world's trade agreements today, nothing comes close in size or significance to the framework established by the WTO. Almost all countries in the world are members of the WTO (to date, 164 countries), which, in a sense, means that the framework of rules set by the WTO is *the* trade agreement of the world.

The WTO is very clear about its mandate. Under the 'Who we are' and 'What we stand for' tabs on the WTO's website, you will find that the WTO is an organization committed to promoting more trade and more free trade. More specifically, the respective tabs on their website say:

> The system's overriding purpose is to help trade flow as freely as possible because this stimulates economic growth and employment and supports the integration of developing countries into the international trading system [...] Lowering trade barriers is an obvious way to encourage trade; these barriers include customs duties (or tariffs) and measures such as import bans or quotas, that restrict quantities selectively.[47]

There is no doubt that the WTO's mandate, in part, is good for the world. International trade is closely tied to poverty reduction and economic development. But a problem arises when free trade benefits some countries more than others.

You won't struggle to find free trade detractors and critics of globalization. In fact, they have been around for centuries. One of the first and most fierce critics of free trade was Alexander Hamilton, a Founding Father of the United States and the country's first Secretary of the Treasury (who I discussed at length in Chapter 1). In his 'Report on Manufactures' submitted to the United States congress in 1791, Hamilton stressed with urgency that his country needed a new approach to international trade, especially with Great Britain.[48] He recognized that Great Britain was miles ahead in areas of innovation and technology, and pointed out that if the United States did not protect its domestic industries through the use of tariffs, it would end up importing advanced technologies from Great Britain at the expense of building up technological capabilities in the United States (especially in manufacturing).

Policymakers in the United States succeeding Hamilton followed his advice. Between 1816 and the end of the Second World War, the United States had the world's highest tariffs on imported manufactures.[49] This is a very important statistic because it implies that the United States—the country many people think of as the bastion of free trade and free markets—actually developed its economy by being a stronghold of protectionism. The argument of Hamilton has lived on, and for good reason. Without active and protectionist trade policies, it is virtually impossible to develop high-tech and high-value industries, which are essential for economic development. The system of free trade that has been promoted particularly since the 1980s keep the global South from catching up with the global North because countries in the global South will be stuck with specializing and producing primary commodities.[50]

It is important to highlight that the WTO acknowledges, in part, that the system of free trade tilts the playing field in favour of those countries specializing in producing and exporting the high-value goods. Therefore, the WTO allows a degree of trade policy 'manoeuvre' for countries in the global South. For example, least developed countries are allowed to use export subsides, whereas other WTO member states are not. But, in its entirety, the WTO cannot hide the fact that it is an organization created by the wealthiest countries, controlled by the wealthiest countries, and, therefore, serving mostly the wealthiest countries. This is why the WTO has come under fire for years for protecting the interests of countries in the global North—often as a result of lobbying efforts by powerful transnational corporations headquartered there—and for limiting the space that countries in the global South have for formulating industrial and trade policies that enable technology transfer and nurture domestic industries (also known as 'policy space').[51] It has actually been documented that transnational corporations based in high-income countries have benefited vastly more than anyone else from WTO proposals implemented since the early 2000s.[52]

In a report I co-authored with Ha-Joon Chang and Muhammad Irfan for the UN Economic Commission for Africa, we looked at WTO regulation on all industrial and trade policies that are normally important to strategically build up domestic technological capabilities within global value chains: tariffs, export subsidies, and regulation on foreign investment.[53] We found that, in summary, the WTO clearly restricts the use of most these policies: the organization outright prohibits export subsidies and requirements on foreign investors to use local content. It is clear that the WTO framework in many ways makes it harder for developing countries to strategically participate in global value chains. But there are a lot of loopholes in this framework that make some industrial and trade policies possible to implement. First, international trade law is more complicated than many people think. Policies that are 'banned' in the WTO framework need, in practice, to be detected and challenged by another country through the dispute settlement mechanism. It can take years before a policy is challenged and ruled illegal. By that time, a 'banned' policy could have had its intended effect. Second, there are a lot of industrial policies that can be safely used if pitched smartly. As a rule of thumb, if a policy does not affect exports or imports, it does not fall directly under WTO law and should be allowed. For example, R&D subsidies, subsides for skills development, and subsidies for the development of disadvantaged regions have hardly ever been challenged. And with respect to regulations on foreign investment, the WTO framework is not very strict on policies aiming to establish joint ventures between domestic and foreign firms or policies that limit foreign equity ownership.

We see now that the WTO is not all that bad. However, although the WTO framework provides some policy space for countries in the global South, it is important to understand that not all agreements within the WTO provide the same amount of policy space. I have now showed how agreements on tariffs, subsidies, and cross-border investments allow for the use of many industrial and trade policies.[54] But the agreement on intellectual property rights within the WTO, formally known as the Agreement on Trade-Related Aspects of Intellectual Property Rights (TRIPS), is not as lenient as the other agreements. It is really important to understand and study TRIPS because this agreement has become a more integral part of the framework for international trade. According to Kevin Gallagher and Richard Kozul-Wright, two prominent experts on global governance, we are entering a new era of trade wars that are less about trade itself and more about the protection of intellectual property, R&D activities, patents, and trade secrets.[55]

In essence, TRIPS ensures that intellectual property (most importantly patents and copyrights) is better protected globally. The idea behind TRIPS is to incentivize more innovation. But the problem with TRIPS is that when innovation is highly skewed globally, it serves to protect the interests of those who are net producers of patentable knowledge.[56] In the global economy today, the global North is a net producer of patentable knowledge, and the global South is a net consumer. However, despite being a net producer of patentable knowledge, the global North (or, rather, companies head-quartered there) rakes in massive profits in many industries without actually producing the things related to their patents, as I showed earlier in this chapter by using the example of the global electronics industry and the global patent distribution in advanced digital technologies. TRIPS exposes the irony of the WTO's mandate: trade should flow freely, especially when it entails cheap goods and services being exported from the South to the North, but technology and knowledge should be protected, especially when there's a chance that it transfers from the North to the South.

A stark reminder of how TRIPS prevents technology transfer to the global South was when COVID-19 vaccines started to be rolled out for public use. In early 2021, there was a big debate between member states of the WTO about whether patents on COVID-19 vaccines should be waived or not. The argument for waiving the patents was that during a global pandemic, it would be inhumane and greedy to prevent developing countries from being able to access the best vaccine recipes. What was the outcome of this debate? More or less all countries in the global North voted to block the waiver on vaccine patents, preventing developing countries from gaining access to the vaccine recipes of companies like Pfizer and AstraZeneca. Having had access to these recipes early on could have saved thousands of lives in the global South, especially in countries with decent manufacturing capacity for vaccines such as India.[57]

So, in many ways, the WTO is broken. How? Because, in practice, the most powerful sovereign states control the organization and try to run it in their interests—which are, in turn, heavily influenced by the interests of powerful transnational corporations. This is not an exaggeration: scholars studying the WTO have, in fact, found that a small group of powerful, high-income countries was deliberately using its power and market influence during the round of trade negotiations that led to the formation of the WTO (the

Uruguay Round) to rewrite the rules of international trade to the advantage of corporations based in its countries.[58] Seeing that this powerful international organization and the most influential trade agreements within it have been established by and for countries and corporations in the global North, it would be useful for countries in the global South to explore alternatives to membership in this organization. Although membership in the WTO remains largely synonymous with actively participating in international trade, some regional alternatives to the WTO are, in fact, emerging. For example, the Regional Comprehensive Economic Partnership (RCEP) trade agreement signed by Asia-Pacific nations in 2020 has become the largest trade bloc in history. It is not entirely made up of countries that would be considered part of the global South, but it certainly does not reflect the WTO's core–periphery structure. The African Continental Free Trade Area (AfCFTA) is another massive trade area founded in 2018 by fifty-four of the fifty-five African Union nations. It is the largest free trade area in the world in terms of the number of participating countries since the establishment of the WTO. These trade agreements may not be a magic bullet for all member countries, but generally, regional and bilateral trade agreements between countries of similar levels of income are more beneficial for the countries that take part in them compared to the framework set by the WTO.

Has the COVID-19 pandemic reversed the globalization of production?

Few things have hit the brakes on globalization like the COVID-19 pandemic. When measures were taken all over the world to keep people at a safe distance from each other, people couldn't go to work and people's consumption patterns changed. Businesses closed, either temporarily or permanently. Even many businesses that were able to keep operations running from a logistics perspective were still unable return to pre-pandemic production volumes from a sales perspective. Why? Because of the global interconnectedness of production and the emergence of complex supply chains and value chains. When the manufacturing process of a single product becomes so complex that it involves dozens of businesses all around world, the process obviously becomes more fragile: the resilience of the entire chain relies on the functioning of each and every part of the chain.[59]

An article published in the *Financial Times* in November 2021 illustrates the global supply and value chain crunch very well.[60] The article explains how the supply chain crisis for paint (yes, paint) impacted the world economy. This is what makes it such a good example. Most of us now understand how, say, the production of a car involves people and businesses from all over the world, but who would have thought that paint has a complex global supply chain? Well, it does. The crisis was mainly caused by a surge in the price of paint, which soared for a number of reasons: the rise in prices of paint ingredients (particularly oil, natural gas, titanium dioxide, and other key chemicals), the Do-It-Yourself (DIY) boom during lock-down, shipping bottlenecks, and truck driver shortages. In turn, the paint crisis hit a bunch of other sectors because, obviously, everyone needs paint—from aerospace, construction, maritime and electronics, to car, pharmaceutical, and textile industries. You name it. The article also details how some of these other sectors were affected by both soaring paint prices and their own supply chain crises. For example, car repair companies in many countries struggled due to soaring paint prices, on the one hand (paint normally makes up a quarter of repair costs for cars), and a surge in demand for car repairs (due to global semiconductor shortages, which slowed down the production of new cars) on the other hand.

It has become clear that all economic crises, even domestic ones and even small ones, now have the ability to rattle the world economy. The crisis caused by the COVID-19 pandemic was a big one, and it rattled the world economy big time. Global trade in goods took a big hit, falling by 10% in 2020, and global flows of foreign direct investments took a humongous hit, falling by 35% in 2020.[61]

It should come as no surprise, then, that the COVID-19 pandemic has accelerated discussions and debates around the future of global value chains.[62] The UN Conference on Trade and Development (UNCTAD) hypothesizes that the COVID-19 pandemic will reinforce existing regionalization and reshoring trends (which I discussed in detail in Chapter 4).[63] The logic behind this is that the pandemic has exposed the fragility of a model characterized by high interdependence between firms across several countries and continents. Reshoring and regionalization of value chains would lead to more self-sufficiency, less fragmented value chains, and a stronger geographical concentration of production. In turn, this would reduce the disruptions that global shocks, like the pandemic, would have on production and consumption. Even in the early stages of the pandemic, we saw countries taking measures to increase self-sufficiency, including introducing temporary export bans on medical equipment, drugs, and food items.[64] Globally, many firms indicate that they will also ramp up the use of automation technology in an effort to reshore and regionalize their value chains. These reshoring and regionalization efforts will not impact all industries in the same way though. It is likely that we will see a more pronounced reorganization of value chains for critical goods, such as medical equipment, pharmaceuticals, and food.

Russia's invasion of Ukraine has exposed the fragility of global interconnectedness in a similar way. Physical blockades and the destruction of productive capacity in Ukraine, on the one hand, and economic sanctions on Russia, on the other hand, raised the global price of commodities of which Russia and Ukraine are key exporters, including oil, natural gas, wheat, barley, pig iron, and fertilizer.[65] The impact was especially painful for countries directly dependent on imports from either Russia or Ukraine—particularly those countries trying to phase out imports from Russia as part of economic sanctions. Many countries in the world also reduced or banned their exports of wheat due to an acute shortage of it.

Economic globalization will surely take on a different form compared to the time before the pandemic and Russia's invasion of Ukraine. Some even predict that we are now witnessing the start of deglobalization or that the COVID-19 pandemic has sounded the death knell of globalization.[66] Rana Foroohar's book, *Homecoming:*

The Path to Prosperity in a Post-Global World, is an important contribution in this respect.[67] It is one of the first post-COVID books to comprehensively make the case that we are entering a new age of economic localization, putting an end to the last half-century of globalization. The book provides detailed and convincing case studies of supply chain disruptions, showing how there is growing policy support for 'made-at-home' initiatives in high-income countries, in particular in the United States.

Foroohar's book is a must-read for understanding how globalization is changing. However, it is scarce on aggregate evidence in support of deglobalization and localization. It cites surveys and interviews with business leaders in support of the localization and regionalization hypothesis—important evidence, for sure—but no macro-level data to make a strong case for 'homecoming'. The lack of aggregate evidence on deglobalization is a common thread among post-COVID deglobalization narratives. We should therefore be cautiously sceptical of these narratives.

A closer look at globalization metrics suggest that globalization is, in fact, back on track, right where it was before the pandemic. In absolute numbers, levels of global trade and global foreign direct investments have, in fact, surpassed pre-pandemic levels.[68] Figure 4.4 illustrates this with reference to how the volume of world trade in goods has changed from 2015 to 2022. The figure shows growth from 2015 to 2020; a sharp fall in the first quarter of 2020, followed by a bounce-back starting in the first quarter of 2021; and continued growth from that point onwards. An important reason for the quick bounce-back to globalization-as-usual is that global value chains and supply chains are complex structures that have been built over many years. Specialization patterns, industrial know-how, capabilities, and tacit knowledge have been developed in specific geographical areas based on a number of factors specific to those areas. While the chains are fragile (the pandemic and the war in Ukraine have clearly proved this), it is not straightforward to remould or rebuild the chains.

Ting-Fang Cheng and Lauly Li have written an eye-opening article on why attempts to 'deglobalize', 'reshore', or 'onshore'

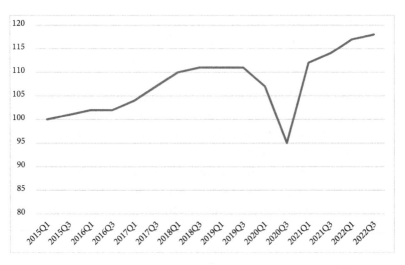

Figure 4.4   Volume of world trade in goods, 2015Q1–2023Q3 (index, 2015Q1 = 100)

Source: https://www.wto.org/english/news_e/pres22_e/pr902_e.htm (accessed 25 March 2023).

semiconductor supply chains (which, for example, the United States is attempting) are mostly futile.[69] They highlight the complexity of the manufacturing process for a myriad of inputs used in semiconductor manufacturing—from ultra-high purity gas cylinder valves to electronic-grade hydrofluoric acid—and how only a few firms in the world are able to manufacture many of these inputs at the highest international standard. These firms have built up capabilities in specific countries that are not easily uprooted from either a technical or political perspective; that is, Japanese, Chinese, or South Korean firms will not simply move to the United States, even if they could from a technical standpoint. The article cites a number of interviews with leading industry experts who warn against efforts in high-income countries to 'reshore' or 'onshore' production in the semiconductor supply chain.

All of this is not to say that events like the COVID-19 pandemic and the war in Ukraine are not having an impact on the nature of globalization. It is important to understand the ways in which events like the COVID-19 pandemic and the war in Ukraine has changed, and is changing, globalization. But it is more important to identify and talk about solutions to the structural and systemic issues in the current era of globalization—issues that have continued during the pandemic, but that the pandemic and the war in Ukraine have unfortunately overshadowed. Globalization in its post-1980s form is still alive and kicking. We cannot let the pandemic and the war in Ukraine distract us from the main problem with the form of globalization we have witnessed in the past few decades: uneven economic exchange between the global South and the global North, benefiting the latter at the expense of the former.

Summary

Over the past few decades, production has become massively fragmented and globally dispersed—a development that is part and parcel of economic globalization since the 1980s. Workers, firms, and sometimes even entire countries have come to occupy segments and niches of so-called global value chains. Industrialization pathways have therefore also changed. For example, countries now specialize in assembling a car rather than making the entire car, or they specialize in producing batteries for phones rather than producing the entire phone.

The globalization of production and the expansion of global value chains have, in some ways, been beneficial for countries in the global South. They have enabled developing countries to join international trade networks more easily, which can boost export earnings and employment in those countries. They have also enabled countries in the global South to join segments of value chains and supply chains, which is easier than building entire industries from scratch. In the age of global value chains, countries need to have fewer capabilities in place in order to be internationally competitive in global industries. I used the example of China to show how strategic participation in global value chains can result in technology transfer from transnational corporations; industrialization of the domestic economy; and, more broadly, economic development.

However, global value chains are far from being a panacea for industrialization and development for countries in the global South. Yes, they have enabled more countries to participate in international trade and reap the benefits of that, but they have also exacerbated power asymmetries in the world economy. Transnational corporations headquartered in the global North—especially the United States—have been able to expand their global reach and power, raking in massive profits at the expense of countries, firms, and workers in the global South. This appropriation of profits is fortified by technological dominance, strong protection of intellectual property rights, favourable trade agreements, low trade barriers, and privileged access to low-cost capital and labour all over the world. This era of dominance by transnational corporations based in the global North has also made it harder for countries in the global South to break into high-value industries and stages of production in value chains. Therefore, even when developing countries are able to enter global value chains, firms and workers participating in these value chains, especially those at the bottom rungs of the chains, barely reap the benefits of doing so. Using the example of the iPhone value chain, I showed how 1.5% of the final retail price goes to those companies and workers who assemble the phone. It should come as no surprise that many workers in global value chains earn wages below what is necessary to have a decent living.

Some scholars now say that we should be talking about global poverty chains, rather than global value chains, and a new form of economic imperialism in the context of globalized production.[70] If we look at global production and export structures over the years, these scholars have a good point. Structural imbalances in the world economy that have existed for a long time remain: the global North still produces and exports high-value goods, and the global South still produces and exports low-value goods.[71] There are a few exceptions, such as China, but even in China, workers still toil for pennies and face awful conditions at the workplace. In fact, incomes in the global North have steadily diverged from incomes in the global South in the age of global value chains.[72]

Even when the COVID-19 pandemic and Russia's invasion of Ukraine rattled economic globalization, the international trading system mostly got back on track in its current form, controlled and dominated by the most powerful transnational corporations. In fact, it exposed how countries and corporations in the global North go to great lengths to protect their technologies from being shared with the global South: most countries in the global North blocked the waiver on COVID-19 vaccine patents in early 2021, a waiver which could have saved thousands of lives. In many ways, then, today's world of global value chains illustrates how poor states are impoverished by being integrated into the world system through a relationship of uneven economic exchange with wealthy states.

5

Ecological breakdown

We are living in an age of ecological breakdown. The Intergovernmental Panel for Climate Change (IPCC)[1] has explicitly stated that human influence, mainly through the emission of greenhouse gases in energy use, has warmed the climate at a rate we have not seen for several thousands of years. Each of the past four decades has been successively warmer than any decade that preceded it since 1850.[2] The consequences of global warming are severe, which rapid changes in our physical environment are already showing us. Heat waves and wildfires are becoming more common; we are witnessing rising sea levels as a consequence of melting sea ice, glaciers, and permafrost; and higher temperatures are also causing more intense storms and other extreme weather events.

Global warming is having a disastrous impact on people's lives. Extreme storms, floods, and heatwaves are now a regular occurrence. In 2017, Category 5 hurricanes—which are normally witnessed once in a generation—rolled in one after another in the Americas, wiping out crops, demolishing houses, and making land uninhabitable. From June to October 2022, heavy floods in Pakistan killed more than 1,500 people and caused damage estimated at US$14.9 billion.[3] The floods, caused by heavier than usual monsoon rains and melting glaciers, were described as the worst in the country's history. Around the same time, thousands of people in Europe died as heatwaves scorched the region. In the United Kingdom, temperatures surpassed 40°C for the first time.

I could outline many more examples showing how global warming has wreaked havoc on humans' and animals' lives. By now, though, most of us are familiar with these stories. And most of us have also been told about horrific future scenarios, for instance, the ongoing

The Future of the Factory. Jostein Hauge, Oxford University Press. © Jostein Hauge (2023).
DOI: 10.1093/oso/9780198861584.003.0006

melting of Himalayan glaciers set to destroy the food and water systems of hundreds of millions of people in South Asia or how rising sea levels could flood or submerge big coastal cities—such as Tokyo, Shanghai, New York, and Kolkata—within this century.

Because the disastrous effects of global warming are manifesting themselves so visibly, it is naturally on everyone's mind. But global warming is only part of ecological breakdown. Another part of ecological breakdown that does not receive as much attention is the plunder of our planet's resources. Think about all the stuff that is extracted from the earth, like plant-based material (biomass), fossil fuels, metals, and non-metallic minerals. In many ways, global warming and resource use are connected because the extraction of most of the earth's resources is also contributing to global warming. A good example of this is fossil fuels used in the energy sector. However, even if we are able to mitigate global warming by switching fully to clean/renewable energy, this does little to reverse deforestation, soil depletion, overfishing, unsustainable extraction of metals and minerals, and mass extinction of species, which all have more to do with the constant growth in material output. The expansion of industrial agriculture and timber logging since 1900 accounts for over half of the world's forest loss in the past 10,000 years.[4] Forty per cent of the planet's soils are now seriously degraded mainly due to industrial agriculture.[5] Ninety per cent of global fish stocks are now depleted or facing collapse because of overfishing.[6] More than 60% of the world's wildlife population has been wiped out since 1970, caused by human destruction of natural habitats.[7]

If we continue to ramp up resource use, which we have been doing at an exponential rate since the mid-1900s, the consequences will be disastrous. It means more deforestation, soil depletion, and overfishing. It means more waste, which means more toxics in our rivers and more plastics in our oceans. It means annihilation of biodiversity and severe disruptions to ecosystems. It also means potentially running out of natural resources that we have started mass-extracting for 'green' products, including the lithium and cobalt that is used in batteries for electric vehicles.

Ecological breakdown is a central challenge to industrialization and manufacturing-led growth. The rapid economic growth, development, and industrialization we have witnessed in the global North since the first Industrial Revolution correlates almost perfectly with global warming and growth in resource use. This is, of course, no coincidence. The nature of industrial production and capital accumulation since the first Industrial Revolution have, by definition, involved unprecedented greenhouse gas emissions and extraction of the earth's resources. There is a strong consensus among political ecologists that industrialization, capital accumulation, and the pursuit of productivity growth have caused, and continue to cause, ecological breakdown. And although we have seen efforts to make production and consumption greener, the rate of expansion combined with expectation of more growth has not slowed down the ecological toll of industrialization and manufacturing-led growth.

In this chapter, I explore the conflict between industrialization and growth, on the one hand, and ecological sustainability on the other hand. The negative impact of industrialization on our planet's ecology is a well-known fact so I do not delve too deeply into mapping out the evidence on the relationship between the two variables. I focus more on the 'So what?' issue, looking at solutions and policy proposals that have been offered to deal with the seeming incompatibility between expanding industrial production and living within planetary boundaries. First, I discuss green paradigms that have emerged, all offering a path for industrialization, development, and growth that is ecologically sustainable and do not require radical transformations to our economic system. These paradigms include green growth, Green New Deals, and green industrial policy. I then discuss degrowth, a perspective that has become incredibly important in discussions on sustainable living. Degrowth does a better job than the green paradigms at identifying the full scale of ecological breakdown, especially by looking at not only energy use but also resource use. Once we understand the full scale of ecological breakdown, and also the fact that a green transition is not keeping up pace with the global growth in energy and resource use, the conflict between industrialization and ecological sustainability becomes clearer, which is why degrowth calls for a drastic reduction in energy and resource use. Towards the end of the chapter, I offer a path forwards based on solutions from both perspectives.

Green paradigms

In October 2018, I was in Oslo, Norway, giving a talk on the role of manufacturing in economic development. It was a special occasion for me because I was presenting together with the famous economic historian, Erik Reinert, who has been an important influence in shaping my work. Erik gave a talk on a similar topic, with a greater historical component of course. During the question-and-answer session, a member of the audience shouted from the back, 'Do you even live on this planet!?'. At first, I was a bit perplexed by the question but soon realized that the question was meant as a sharp critique of our talks' inadequate coverage of ecological challenges. Whereas I was struggling to understand the question immediately and needed time to gather my thoughts, Erik straightaway knew what the question hinted at and gave a very interesting answer.

He first asked the audience if anyone could tell him about the nature of the greatest environmental concern in London and New York in the 1890s. No one, of course, knew, including myself, so Erik went on to explain that it was horse shit. Literally. It is popularly referred to as the 'Great horse manure crisis of 1894' because of the piles of horse manure that had gathered in large urban areas like London and New York. The crisis was serious not only because of the amount of manure a horse produces (10–15 kg per day for a grown horse) but also because the manure attracted a huge number of flies, which then spread typhoid fever and other diseases. In an attempt to figure out solutions to this problem, a ten-day urban planning conference was convened in New York in 1898. But the conference was reportedly abandoned after three days because none of the delegates could come up with solutions that didn't involve bringing in more horses to remove the horse manure.[8]

As Erik arrived at the turning point of his story, explaining how the horse manure crisis was solved, people started to realize where he was getting at. The solution was obviously cars! With time, cars came to replace horses and horse carriages in the streets of New York and London. The horse shit crisis was soon buried in the past rather than New York and London being buried in horse shit. The point of Erik's story was that technological progress, specifically in industrial production, solved an important ecological problem. This is not to say that industrialization is not, and has not been, harmful to our planet's ecology, as Erik acknowledged. But part of the solution to the problem of ecological breakdown can be found in industrial production and technological innovation. The progress we have made in producing renewable energy in the past few decades is directly linked to the manufacturing sector. Wind turbines, photovoltaic cells (solar panels), nuclear power plants, and hydroelectric dams are a few such examples. The manufacturing sector has also played a central role in technological innovation for water purification and waste management, such as in water filtration systems, desalination plants, composting toilets, sewage systems, and bioreactors. And now that the car has become one of the main culprits behind ecological breakdown, rather than horses, the manufacturing sector is playing a crucial role in reinventing transport devices that are less reliant on fossil fuels in their energy use. Electric vehicles are the most famous example.

Green growth

These green technological solutions no doubt involve economic growth. This implies that economic growth can, in theory, be ecologically sustainable. In fact, if we accept that solutions within the sphere of industrial production are necessary to deal with ecological breakdown, some economic growth is necessary to save the planet. But given that a lot of economic growth has, in reality, been the culprit behind ecological breakdown, we need to discuss ways to make growth greener. Over the years, this topic has received more attention alongside greater concerns about ecological breakdown, and the term 'green growth' has been borne out of such discussions. Green growth as an agenda was largely pushed by the Organisation for Economic Co-operation and Development (OECD), the World Bank, and the United Nations Environment Programme (UNEP) in the early 2010s and has, by now, become mainstream.[9] Unlike the term 'sustainable development', green growth is a more focused term and more or less self-explanatory, which explains its popular appeal. The idea behind green growth is simply that economic growth needs to move in a direction where it becomes more ecologically sustainable.

The literature on green growth is rich with examples and ideas whereby growth, development, and ecological sustainability go hand in hand. For example, the World Bank has outlined how policies that focus on ecological sustainability as a priority can have positive effects on growth and development: (i) preserving our ecology will make people healthier and therefore more productive; (ii) food production depends on healthy soil and ecosystems so preserving our ecology can generate more stable and higher incomes in the agricultural sector and in fisheries; (iii) prioritizing green technologies is in itself green growth and, in some instances, also more cost-efficient as measured by market prices.[10] Another important channel through which economic growth and green policies are connected is through job creation. The economist Robert Pollin suggests that a heavier focus on green energy will have a positive effect on job creation because green energy sectors absorb more labour than the fossil fuel sectors, the latter of which are highly capital-intensive.[11] A recent study supports this claim, finding that more jobs are created in green energy sectors compared to the fossil fuel sectors per US$ invested in the respective sectors.[12]

Green New Deals

Green growth is not the only green paradigm that has gathered steam in recent years. Its close cousin, the Green New Deal, is also becoming popular. Green New Deal proposals are sweeping public policy packages aiming to address climate change and global warming while, at the same time, creating jobs and tackling economic inequality.[13] The term is a reference to the New Deal, a government programme launched in the United States in the 1930s focusing on public works, finance reforms and regulations in the aftermath of the Great Depression. It was enforced and overseen by President Franklin D. Roosevelt, who, partly because of the success of the New Deal, is one of the most popular presidents in US history. Green New Deal proposals have a strong association with progressive politics, particularly in the United States, where the term originated. Green Party candidates in the United States have been running on Green New Deal platforms since the early 2010s, and in 2019, the Democrats Alexandria Ocasio-Cortez and Ed Markey attempted to get legislation passed for a Green New Deal in the US Senate.

Other than being massive public reform programmes, what exactly do the Green New Deal programmes entail? The Green New Deal proposed by Alexandria Ocasio-Cortez and Ed Markey in 2019 is instructive to look at because this is the Green New Deal that has received most attention (to some, this is known as *the* Green New Deal).[14] The overarching aim of this deal was, naturally, that it should be green. More specifically, the main goal of the plan was to bring greenhouse gas emissions in the United States down to net zero by 2030 and meet 100% of energy demand in the country through clean and renewable energy sources by 2030. Further to this, a massive pillar of the programme was environmental justice and social justice. Justice was emphasized because frontline and vulnerable communities are more likely to be affected by climate change and because major shifts in energy sectors will impact the lives of people in these communities more than they will impact the lives of the rich. The focus on justice was reflected in many of the Deal's pillars, including restoring ecosystems, identifying sources of pollution, cleaning up hazardous waste, investing in public transportation systems, upgrading buildings to achieve energy efficiency and safety, and providing affordable electricity. A third pillar of the programme was huge amounts of public investment. Key investment areas highlighted included renewable energy, the manufacturing sector (i.e. investments to make it greener), and transportation systems. The focus on investment in clean, renewable energy as well as achieving better energy efficiency is a pillar in most Green New Deal proposals. In addition to many overlaps between this specific Green New Deal, other such deals outline revenue generation to pay for public investments with a focus on carbon taxes, transfers from military budgets, green bond purchases, government procurement, and investment subsidies.[15]

Green industrial policy

We now see a few commonalities emerging from the green paradigms I have discussed: (i) change to the status quo of the global economic system is needed, involving a heavier focus on ecological sustainability and green growth; (ii) the manufacturing sector has to play an indispensable role in a green transition, both through offering new, green technological solutions and through making existing energy systems and solutions greener; (iii) state action, involvement, and investment is crucial to achieve a green transition. All these three points can be said to fall under the rubric of 'green industrial policy', which, just like green growth and Green New Deals, is a term becoming more popular and central in discussions on ecological sustainability.[16]

In short, the rationale behind green industrial policy is that because private markets cannot solve the problems caused by ecological breakdown by themselves, state intervention and action is necessary. Of course, one could argue that private markets have never been, nor are they, the natural state of affairs and that industrial policy has always been indispensable in developing an economy's productive and industrial structure (which I showed in Chapter 2). In this sense, green industrial policy is not a fix to a problem that another mechanism would ideally solve (in this case, private markets) but rather a core player from the get-go. Another important rationale for green industrial policy is that a policy focus on industry, manufacturing, and infrastructure is essential to achieve a green transition. Like the green growth and Green New Deal paradigms, green industrial policy focuses heavily on how to reduce greenhouse gas emissions through new and renewed energy systems, energy infrastructure, and energy efficiency.

In the fight to preserve our ecology, studies on green industrial policy are useful in many ways. First, they provide a range of industry case studies to draw inspiration from, and learn lessons from, in working towards a green transition. To name a few, you will find extensive studies on public investments in renewable energy in Equador and Morocco, state-led electric vehicles programmes in China, and ethanol policy in Brazil.[17] Second, work on green industrial policy provides insight into the nitty gritty of green policies, including carbon taxes, feed-in tariffs, research and development (R&D) support, subsidized credit, and public procurement. This is important knowledge to have in order to really understand how green policies work in practice. Third, work on green industrial policy has made an effort to identify opportunities for countries in the global South to gain a competitive edge in sectors and industries that contain a new generation of technologies which no country in the global North has a massive competitive edge in yet.[18] This is often referred to as taking advantage of 'windows of opportunities' or 'technological leapfrogging'. For example, countries in the global South could directly leapfrog into building capabilities in green energy rather than going through the same, traditional industrialization route that countries in the global North have done.

In short, the paradigms on green growth, Green New Deals, and green industrial policy offer useful ways to meet the challenge of ecological breakdown. They all recognize that the status quo cannot continue if we want to save our planet, and they all offer ideas and policy proposals to push innovation, technology, and economic development in a direction that preserves our planet's ecology. However, a problem with these green paradigms is that they remain overly focused on how we can mitigate global warming. Ecological breakdown is not just about global warming, and, in formulating solutions, we need to look beyond green energy and reductions to greenhouse gas emission. Ecological breakdown is also happening due to unprecedented plundering of our planet's resources caused by human beings, that is, the material footprint we leave behind. A second problem with these green paradigms is that they do not properly address the issue that green solutions are not keeping pace with ever-increasing consumption and production. The supply of clean energy is growing, but the supply of dirty energy is growing even faster, and absolute levels of greenhouse gas emissions keep going up every year. We need to confront these two problems of the green paradigms more seriously, but the discussion then becomes more complicated. Why? Because we are then more forcefully challenged to rethink the idea that economic growth is good and sustainable.

The case for degrowth

The rise of degrowth

Economic growth has long been viewed as an essential component of economic development because it raises the material standards of living for most people (when the growth is widely shared). Economic growth has meant technological innovation in all areas of society, better health, better infrastructure, better housing, and better and more jobs. Countries that have achieved higher rates of economic growth over time and higher levels of income for its citizens are also viewed as more 'developed' countries. Achieving high rates of economic growth has thus come to be regarded as equivalent to becoming more prosperous, healthy, and technologically advanced.

Growth is measured by increases to a country's gross domestic product (GDP)—in short, the market value of goods and services produced by a country. Therefore, growth in GDP has become regarded as the alfa and omega in gauging a country's economic success, an end in itself. However, this is not how the 'inventor' of GDP, Simon Kuznets, envisaged it. While Kuznets saw GDP as a useful metric to capture the total economic output of a country and as a means to the end of raising living standards, he warned that it should never be confused with well-being.[19] Kuznets's warning has been taken more seriously in recent years, and although countries keep pursuing growth, it is largely accepted by now that development, prosperity, and well-being is not just about growth. These things are also about 'human development', a term and approach pioneered by Amartya Sen and Martha Nussbaum in the 1980s focusing on aspects of social justice, freedom, good health, and education not captured in the GDP metric.[20] Building on the human development approach, a range of well-being indexes have now been developed which are also putting a heavier emphasis on inequality and ecology.[21]

Economic growth clearly does not capture all aspects of well-being. It often neglects activities that are essential in all societies, including housework, voluntary work, and subsistence farming. In fact, growth can sometimes be bad for society: the development of nuclear warheads and financial speculation contribute to economic growth. But nowhere is the negative impact of growth felt more strongly than in the area of ecology. More growth often means more global warming; more unsustainable extraction of the earth's resources; and more destruction of land, oceans, and wildlife habitat. The incompatibility between economic growth and ecological sustainability has been documented for some time now but has only recently become more mainstream. Even the IPCC now explicitly highlights this incompatibility:

> GDP is a poor metric of human well-being, and climate policy evaluation requires better grounding in relation to decent living standards [. . .] The working of economic systems under a well-being driven rather than GDP driven paradigm requires better understanding.[22]

It should come as no surprise that voices calling for an end to the pursuit of growth in light of ecological breakdown are taken more seriously. Grounded in work published in the 1970s highlighting the limits to growth,[23] the degrowth perspective collects many such voices. According to a 2017 article reviewing literature on this perspective, degrowth has evolved within a decade from an activist movement into a multidisciplinary paradigm.[24] In discussions on sustainable economic growth and development, the degrowth perspective now has a seat at the table. And when it doesn't, it should. What exactly is degrowth though? In their recent book, *The Case for Degrowth*, Giorgos Kallis and co-authors say that 'the case for degrowth is a case for stopping the pursuit of growth and for reorienting lives and societies toward wellbeing'.[25] In his article, 'What Does Degrowth Mean? A Few Points of Clarification', Jason Hickel defines degrowth as 'a planned reduction of energy and resource use designed to bring the economy back into balance'.[26] The largest empirical survey of degrowth proponents to date, launched at a 2014 conference in Leipzig, found a consensus around degrowth being fundamentally critical of growth, capitalism, and industrialism.[27] This distinguishes degrowth from the green paradigms discussed earlier in the chapter, which are all more vague about the need to transform capitalism and reduce excess consumption and production.

The full scale of ecological breakdown

One of the great things about work on degrowth is that it does a very good job at identifying ecological breakdown. The terms 'energy use' and 'resource use' are important in this respect. Discussions on global warming and climate change focus mostly on energy use. This is why most of us have seen figures illustrating how much the planet is warming up or how much CO_2 emissions are increasing over time. Resource use is equally, if not more, important. A metric often used to capture resource use is 'material footprint'. This metric measures the weight of all the stuff extracted from the earth by human beings, calculated by adding up the extraction of biomass, fossil fuels, metal ores, and non-metal ores. Think about all the trees that are cut down, coal that is burned, rare-earth metals extracted, coral reefs destroyed, and animals killed by human activity. Material footprint also accounts for ecological damage caused by mass production of goods in the renewable energy industry, for instance, solar panels and electric vehicles.

The literature on degrowth puts material footprint at centre stage, and rightly so. Metrics that inform us about global warming are important, but they don't tell us that much about deforestation, soil depletion, overfishing, mass extinction of species, depletion of metals, and, more generally, excess use of the earth's resources. Material footprint accounts for these things and, at the same time, captures climate change (because most human activities resulting in greenhouse gas emissions are a result of using and extracting the earth's materials and resources). This is why metrics on resource use account for more than 90% of the variation in environmental damage indicators.[28]

A quick dive into the degrowth literature will show you data on material footprint[29]—disturbing data because growth in material footprint globally looks more like an exponential rather than a linear function. From 1900 to 1950, global material footprint doubled from 7 billion tonnes to 14 billion tonnes. But from 1950 to 2020, global material footprint exploded, growing sevenfold from 14 billion tonnes to 98 billion tons (see Figure 5.1). Scientists consider the

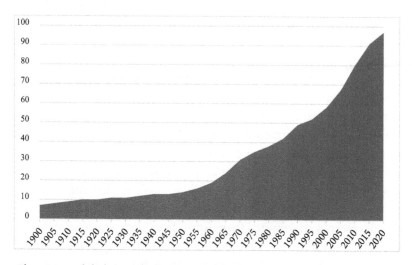

Figure 5.1 Global material footprint (billion tonnes), 1900–2020

Source: Author, based on data from https://www.materialflows.net (accessed 25 March 2023).

maximum sustainable threshold to be at 50 billion tons.[30] Not only is our plunder of the earth's resources unsustainable but also we are actually far past the threshold of sustainable extraction.

The manufacture of renewable energy devices is a great example of how industrial production geared towards mitigating global warming is a double-edged sword: on the one hand, the use of such devices reduces greenhouse gas emissions, but, on the other hand, the production of these devices leaves a significant material footprint. There is therefore a strange irony to the climate change movement because policies to reduce global warming will require ramping up resource use massively. In order to reduce global greenhouse gas emissions to net zero by 2050 (a goal set out in the Paris Agreement), global demand for rare-earth minerals and metals will have to increase between 300% and 1,000%. At this point already, Europe is facing a critical shortage of clean energy metals. A report coming out of KU Leuven estimates that in order to meet its clean energy goals by 2050, Europe will require thirty-five times more lithium and between six and twenty-seven times the amount of rare earth metals compared to the consumption of these in 2020.[31]

Industry-specific studies tell a similar story. In 2019, a group of British scientists submitted a letter to the United Kingdom's Committee on Climate Change outlining concerns about the damaging ecological impact of electric vehicle production. They pointed out that replacing the world's fleet of current vehicles with electric vehicles will require an explosive increase in mining: the annual global extraction of neodymium and dysprosium will have to go up 70%, the annual global extraction of copper will have to double, and the annual global extraction of cobalt will have to increase fourfold.[32] We are already seeing how the earth's cobalt reserves are becoming strained. Almost all of the world's cobalt is currently mined in one country, the Democratic Republic of Congo (DRC). When cobalt reserves are emptied there (or if they become unavailable for export), we will have to start mining it from the deep seabed. Deep seabed mining of cobalt and other metals (lithium and nickel) is already having a destructive impact on deep sea ecosystems and biodiversity and can have further negative knock-on effects on global food security, fisheries, and nutrient cycles in the deep seabed. This is why many environmental organizations, scientists, and politicians are calling for a global moratorium on all deep seabed mining activities.[33]

This is bad enough, but unfortunately it gets worse as I haven't made much mention of lithium mining, which is when things turn really bad. Lithium is the primary ingredient in lithium batteries, one of the most popular batteries today. Most devices based on renewable energy are highly dependent on these batteries because renewable energy devices need to store a lot of energy. This is the case not only for electric vehicles but also for windmills and solar panels. It is estimated that we need a 2,700% increase in lithium extraction compared to current levels if we are to power up the world with renewable energy.[34] This would have to involve way more deep seabed mining, which would have even more devastating impacts on deep seabed ecosystems. Extracting and refining lithium also requires a huge amount of water, which is already tapping out water supplies for many countries and farmers in the global South. I will leave it up to your imagination to predict what will happen when the lithium boom starts for real.

An additional, and very important, feature of ecological breakdown often overlooked in the mainstream literature is that growth in renewable energy supply is not keeping up with growth in aggregate energy demand. Sales of electric vehicles are growing but so are sales of sport utility vehicles (SUVs). Solar, wind, and hydropower are growing quickly but so is the extraction of fossil fuels. According to data from the International Energy Agency, the share of fossil fuels in final energy demand didn't budge from 2010 to 2020, staying firmly at 80%.[35] This is because energy demand is ratcheting up year by year and so are global CO_2 emissions, whose absolute levels are steadily climbing year by year. Clean and green substitutes are necessary but clearly not sufficient. One of the key takeaways from the work on degrowth is therefore that we fundamentally need to change the way we live, discarding our obsession with growth of resource use, growth of energy use, capital accumulation, and hence growth of GDP.

The degrowth agenda

If we accept the premise of degrowth, what kind of policies does this call for? This depends on who you ask. Scholars who work on degrowth do not make up a homogenous entity and advocate in different ways for ecological sustainability. Policy proposals naturally differ. However, it is still possible to make a few generalizations. Degrowth generally welcomes policies presented by the green paradigms I discussed, and in many ways, they overlap. For example, Green New Deal proposals and degrowth are grounded in progressive and socialist principles advocating for social inclusion and community support, decommodification of public goods, redistribution, and green public finance and tax programmes.

But whereas degrowth accepts these green policies as necessary, they are deemed insufficient. The main difference between the green paradigms and degrowth lies in the sustainability of growth: degrowth more explicitly outlines a strategy to decrease energy and resource use. A transition towards a post-capitalist world is at the heart of this strategy. Degrowth sees capitalism as a core culprit behind excess energy, material, and resource use because the search for more profit and capital accumulation—with disregard for ecological sustainability—is a fundamental part of the capitalist system.

Therefore, degrowth pushes hard for reclaiming the commons, calling for an end to the for-profit organization of the economy in areas such as housing, utilities, transportation, land, finance, and health (all areas that actually used to be part of the commons before they became subject to a massive privatization drive starting in the 1980s). Degrowth also calls more forcefully for scaling down ecologically damaging activities in the private sector, for instance, advertising, planned obsolescence in industrial production, and food waste. While this is good for the planet, it is not necessarily good for all aspects of the economy. There is a recognition that output will probably decrease and unemployment rates increase as a consequence of such a strategy. The remedy suggested by degrowth is a reduction in working hours and the introduction of universal basic income

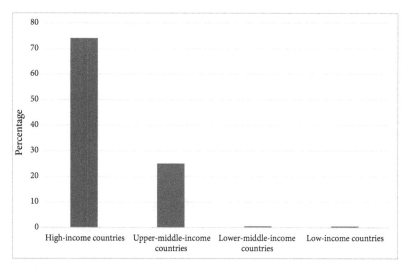

Figure 5.2 Shares of global excess resource use, 1970–2017
Source: Author, based on data from Hickel et al. (2022b).

and universal basic services. This will allow work to be distributed more evenly among the population and guarantees basic income and services in order for people to live a healthy and decent life.

It is important to stress that degrowth calls for a reduction in energy and resource use mainly in the global North rather than in the global South. The reason for this is simple: today's high-income countries are the ones responsible for ecological breakdown and they continue to be the main culprits. According to an article published in *Lancet Planetary Health*, high-income countries were responsible for 74% of global excess resource use between 1970 and 2017 (see Figure 5.2).[36] Upper-middle-income countries were responsible for 25% (most of this is China). Lower-middle-income countries and low-income countries were responsible for a mere 1% combined of global excess resource use in this time period, even though they account for roughly half of the world's population.

Keep in mind that the starting point for this study is 1970. Prior to 1970, excess resource and energy use can be almost entirely attributed to the global North as the material footprint left by the global South in this time period is negligible in relative terms. The authors of the *Lancet* study explicitly underscore this issue. They stress that if responsibility for excess resource use were to be calculated in a manner that accounted for patterns of industrial development in the 1800s and the first half of the 1900s, global excess resource use of the United States and the European Union (EU) would be higher than their results suggest and that of countries in the global South would be lower.

Towards the edge of the cliff: Trade-offs and challenges

Industrialization has historically involved an expansion in economic output, capital accumulation, and growth in greenhouse gas emissions and resource use. This continues to be the case. Does this mean that ecologically sustainable industrialization is a contradiction? Not necessarily. Remember that the culprits behind ecological breakdown are today's high-income countries. They are the ones responsible for ecological overshoot both in the past and in the present. Clearly, they should be the ones to pay the price. Hence, degrowth calls for a reduction in energy and resource use in the global North, not the global South. Industrial policy in the global South should therefore have more 'ecological policy space' than industrial policy in the global North. But many challenges remain.

The challenge of export-oriented industrialization

We should accept that countries in the global South increase their material footprint (to some degree) as they industrialize. But if we advocate strongly for degrowth in the global North at the same time, this creates a problem, which is that global demand for exports from the global South drops. More specifically, industrialization in the global South based on exports to the global North becomes challenging. In the field of development economics, the strong relationship between industrialization, development, and exports to high-income countries has become a stylized fact, so much so that terms like export-oriented industrialization, export-oriented development, and export-led growth have become staple terms. Countries that transformed their economies from low income to high income rapidly in the twentieth century all followed an export-oriented industrialization strategy. The most famous cases were the Asian tigers (Hong Kong, Singapore, South Korea, and Taiwan), who all heavily depended on demand from high-income countries, in particular the United States.

In South Korea, exports were so heavily stressed during the early phases of industrialization that President Park Chung-hee even called it the economic lifeline of the country in his State of the Nation speech in 1965. In the 1970s, the zenith of South Korea's industrialization boom, 50% of the country's exports went to the United States.[37] The more recent example is China, whose economic growth, industrialization, and exports of manufactured goods—especially to the United States and Europe—show an almost perfect positive correlation with one another between 1980 and 2010. It is no coincidence that China has lifted more people out of poverty in the past forty years than the rest of the world put together and, at the same time, has become the world's factory, so to speak.

It is, of course, conceivable (and probable) that new models of industrialization and new export destinations emerge. If we follow the premise that high-income countries will degrow their economies, low-income countries in the global South could export their products to upper-middle-income countries that are emerging as consumer destinations. Patterns of world trade have indeed been shifting along such lines, and several middle-income countries in Asia are now becoming important consumer markets in the world economy.[38] This means that African countries can, in theory, industrialize by exporting manufactured goods to East Asia. But there is no guarantee that this direction of trade will be any more ecologically sustainable than South/North trade in the past. In fact, as China has emerged as a more important consumer market in the world economy, its ecological overshoot has ramped up. Between 1970 and

2017, China accounted for 15% of the world's ecological overshoot. This is the second largest national ecological overshoot in the world in this time period after the United States (27%).[39]

An honest call for degrowth in countries that are responsible for ecological breakdown will therefore have to call for more regional trade between countries in the global South and more domestic-based consumption in the global South. This is, in fact, something that scholars from the degrowth perspective call for, not only because the export-oriented model is no longer as feasible when countries of higher income degrow their economies but also because community-centred living with less trade crossing borders is more ecologically sustainable.[40] However, these solutions do not properly own up to the simple fact that countries in the global South that shelve export-oriented industrialization strategies will experience slower levels of poverty reduction and economic development. This is not only because revenue generation and job creation through exports will slow down but also because technological development and innovation—cornerstones of economic development—happen through exports to countries of higher income. Becoming internationally competitive in sophisticated industries is about getting market shares in consumer markets with high purchasing power. Ultimately, we have to recognize the trade-offs involved here: degrowth in high-income and upper-middle-income countries and less trade between the global South and the global North will have some negative knock-on effects for economic development in the global South at large.

The challenge of implementing the degrowth agenda

In light of this evidence, if we still accept that degrowth is a good strategy to pursue, there is the issue of actually getting countries in the global North to degrow their economies. A big obstacle here is that the countries that are causing ecological breakdown suffer disproportionately less from it. This is not because ecological breakdown isn't impacting high-income countries but rather because these countries have the money, power, and technology to mitigate many of the negative effects. There simply isn't as much urgency for high-income countries to reorganize their economies in an ecologically sustainable way as there is for low-and middle-income countries. Seeing that this is a global problem, we would ideally have an international body capable of enforcing environmental and ecological standards. But we don't. The world economy is, in many ways, a structure in which sovereign states compete against one another, cooperating only when it serves them. This is why it is so difficult to achieve meaningful cooperation on climate action and ecological matters.

The Paris Agreement adopted in 2015 was a good step in the right direction, but, like most other international climate initiatives, it has been mostly talk with little meaningful action. Global greenhouse gas emissions and material footprint have steadily increased since 2015. Most scientists have, by now, concluded that reducing greenhouse gas emissions by 50% by 2030—a core aim of the Paris Agreement—is an illusion. This is why the famous climate activist, Greta Thunberg, famously quipped at the youth climate summit in 2021, 'Build back better. Blah, blah, blah. Green economy. Blah, blah, blah. Net zero by 2050. Blah, blah, blah.'[41]

It's probably a better bet that countries take action based on domestic rather than international pressure. Ultimately, politicians are elected to represent *their* people, not other countries' people. Our hope should be that people all over the world elect and put pressure on their leaders to take urgent action to limit ecological breakdown. More people than ever care about environmental and ecological issues. In a survey of more than 80,000 people across forty countries, researchers at the University of Oxford found that 70% of people think that climate change is a 'very, or extremely, serious problem'. Fewer than 3% said climate change is not serious at all.[42] Fortunately, green parties are rising, and green policies are becoming more prominent on political and policy agendas around the world. But even though a record number of people care about environmental and ecological issues, the type of action we need is not happening fast enough. There's still mostly blah, blah, blah.

One reason why we are not seeing action to mitigate ecological breakdown fast enough is because the economic system we have adopted—more specifically, capitalism—makes it difficult to achieve. This is actually a core argument of degrowth. The critique of capitalism coming from this perspective is well summarized in a *Monthly Review* article entitled 'For an Ecosocialist Degrowth'. The article, bearing resemblance to a manifesto, combines views from degrowth and ecosocialist communities. It starts out with the following argument as the first of its eight pillars:

> Capitalism cannot exist without growth. It needs a permanent expansion of production and consumption, accumulation of capital, maximization of profit. This process of unlimited growth, based on the exploitation of fossil fuels since the eighteenth century, is leading to ecological catastrophe, climate change, and threatens the extinction of life on the planet. The twenty-six UN Climate Change Conferences of the last thirty years manifest the total unwillingness of the ruling elites to stop the course toward the abyss.[43]

The manifesto explicitly calls for radical solutions to deal with the root of the problem. And you can't deny that there's a pretty good case to be made for radical solutions when over two dozen UN climate change conferences have done nothing to reverse ecological breakdown. We have actually been pushed closer towards the edge of the cliff while these conferences have taken place. An important proposition in the manifesto is that we need democratic ecological planning. The idea is that people, rather than corporations, should exercise direct power in democratically determining what is to be produced, how, and how much. A second important proposition in the manifesto is that we cannot accept a mere reduction of ecological harmful activities—some of them actually have to be suppressed, like coal-fired activities and advertisement.

These propositions are well intentioned and should be taken seriously, but given that the clock is ticking fast, we need to talk about measures that are practically and politically feasible to implement *right now*, within the structure of the current system. Some degrowth proponents actually identify their paradigm as being partly a utopian project rather than a practical policy agenda, meant to ignite discussions about alternative futures.[44] A recent paper in *Sustainability* provides a more practical policy perspective based on a review of both degrowth and green growth literatures. The authors conclude that, 'the often radical degrowth proposals suffer from many uncertainties and risks [. . .] It is very unlikely that alternative welfare conceptions can convince a critical mass of countries to go along with the degrowth agenda.'[45] The paper goes on to endorse policies that are more aligned with the green paradigms, including green investment packages, green innovation, and carbon taxes. However, these staple green paradigm policies have featured heavily in many major economies over the past decade without having the impact we need to see if we are to save our planet. But, on the other hand, if degrowth is a utopian project, is there any hope for change in the present?

Where green paradigms and degrowth meet: Possible policy pathways

My analysis might seem a bit bleak at this point. I have pointed out that even if we allow countries in the global South more ecological policy space, export-oriented industrialization and development is a trickier path if countries in the global North degrow at the same time. And if, for the sake of the argument, we overlook this challenge for a moment, is it even realistic for countries in the global North to embark on degrowth strategies in the short term, given the meagre political power to support this and propositions that, while well intentioned, are practically challenging to implement? My intention is not to paint a bleak picture but rather to highlight trade-offs and challenges involved in this process. Luckily, there are some propositions that are not too challenging to implement—propositions spinning out from the degrowth literature that find support from green growth, Green New Deals, and green industrial policy.

One such proposition is to identify the most ecologically destructive activities and industries and start scaling them down. The advertising industry is one of them. The explosive growth in resource use since 1970 has not been driven by fulfilling people's actual needs and wants, it has been driven by the advertising industry pushing onto people what they don't need and don't want. Scaling down the advertising industry is not rocket science. We already have regulations in place restricting where, how, and what companies can advertise, now we just have to make these regulations tighter. We also need to scale down more specific industries. Some are obvious: the fossil fuel industry and the aviation industry. Others are not so obvious, for instance, the beef industry. I mentioned in the introduction that the expansion of industrial agriculture is one of the main causes of rapid deforestation and soil degradation worldwide. The beef industry is the driver of this: almost 60% of agricultural land in the world is connected to the beef industry through grazing and animal feed production. Beef does not represent a necessary component of a healthy diet, certainly not to the extent that it is consumed by people in North America and Europe. A simple and healthy change of diet away from beef and a gradual scaling down of the beef industry could make a big difference to the planet.

A second proposition is to target and scale down the consumption habits of the rich—the people causing the most ecological damage. It is those with the largest quantities of wealth who pollute the most and leave the largest material footprints. The aviation industry, which we all know is a big culprit behind greenhouse gas emissions, is a good case in point. In the United Kingdom, 70% of all flights were taken by 15% of adults according to a 2014 government survey.[46] The numbers are even more shocking when we enter the territory of the super-rich and their playthings. A study looking at the ten celebrities with the highest private jet emissions found that their average CO_2 emissions halfway through 2022 was more than 3,300 metric tons.[47] Remember, this is only emissions from their jets. To put into perspective how shockingly high this number is, the average person's CO_2 emissions globally is 7 metric tons, which includes all activities throughout a full year. Superyachts are equally bad. An analysis by the German media company, *Deutsche Welle*, found that the top twenty billionaires in the world emitted an average of 8,000 metric tons of CO_2 in 2018, of which two-thirds were caused by superyachts.[48] Keep in mind that these statistics on jet and yacht emissions do not account for all the resource and energy use going into the production and maintenance of these wasteful and useless items. There is generally strong public support to clamp down on this kind of wasteful consumption and activity. Canada has already introduced luxury taxes on private jets and super yachts. There is nothing stopping other governments from following in Canada's footsteps.

A third proposition is to make industrial production more ecologically sustainable by incentivizing the manufacture of long-lasting products. Planned obsolescence has unfortunately become a widespread feature of capitalist production. Take smartphones as an example. Between 2010 and 2019, smartphone manufacturers sold a total of 13 billion smartphones. In 2020, less than 3 billion of them were in use. The growth of the use-and-dispose culture is not just subject to smartphones; we see it everywhere: computers, beauty products, toys, furniture, and clothes (think about the rise of fast fashion). How can we end planned obsolescence? It's not actually that hard. If manufacturers in the electronics industry were held to guarantees of at least ten years, we would see more long-lasting products. This would go a long way to reducing resource and energy use.

A fourth proposition is a shift from individual to community-centred living. This goes far beyond being some hippie-inspired idea as we are already seeing lots of countries starting to disincentivize the use of, for example, cars in big, urban centres. Oslo has made large parts of its city centre inaccessible for cars, London has introduced ultra-low emission zones and congestion charge zones for cars, and Milan has vastly expanded its bicycle network. A massive shift towards more public transport is the big one here, but sharing more land, recreational areas, and housing is also important to reduce our material footprint. In order to make this happen, we need to get these things back in the hands of the public again, reversing the privatization of public goods and services that has taken place across many countries over the past fifty years. Housing has become especially bad. Property markets now cater to landlords, developers, and financiers rather than to people's housing needs. Houses are now seen as a good for generating returns on investment rather than places where people can live affordably, sustainably, and comfortably. In many parts of the world, owning property versus not owning property has become the factor determining whether you are on the path to prosperity or a path to poverty. The deregulation of the housing market is opening up for billionaires to horde property, which, in turn, paves the way for rent hikes, growing deficits of social and cooperative housing, and unsustainable housing solutions. In England, social housebuilding is at its lowest rate in decades: since 1991, there has been an average annual net loss of 24,000 social homes.[49]

All the policies I have outlined above need to be implemented alongside the staple policies of the green paradigms, which focus heavily on clean energy and more energy efficiency. The idea is that, together, these policies reduce both greenhouse gas emissions and our material footprint. And let me rehash that it is mainly the responsibility of countries in the global North to urgently implement green policies and degrowth policies. There is absolutely nothing wrong with countries in the global South embarking on a green transition (it should be welcomed), but these countries should have more ecological policy space.

Summary

We are living in an age of ecological breakdown. This is visible in many ways. The first, which we can see on TV and read about in the news every day, is climate change, caused by human-induced greenhouse gas emissions that are warming up the planet. The effects are manifesting themselves so visibly at this point that extreme storms, heatwaves, and wildfires are a regular occurrence. The second part of ecological breakdown, which does not make it to the news as often, is the overuse of the earth's resources (often referred to as resource use or material use). This is part and parcel of climate change because the extraction and overuse of the earth's resources, especially in the fossil-fuel industry, is contributing to greenhouse gas emissions. But the overuse of the earth's resources is causing ecological disaster beyond climate change. Deforestation, soil depletion, overfishing, unsustainable extraction of metals and minerals, and mass extinction of species will all keep growing if we stay on the same trajectory of resource use, even if we switch fully to clean energy.

Industrialization, global warming, and overuse of the earth's resources have historically been three peas in a pod. We only started to witness explosive growth rates in output, fossil-fuel driven energy use, and resource use after the onset of the first Industrial Revolution in the late eighteenth century. International climate agreements even have benchmarks to compare today's levels of global warming to 'pre-industrial levels' because this is the last time we can confidently say that we lived within planetary boundaries. Many political ecologists are now in active opposition to policies that promote industrialization and productivity growth.

The negative impact that industrialization has on resource and energy use should come as no surprise as manufacturing by definition involves transforming raw materials and resources into finished products, requiring energy. People and societies did, of course, manufacture things before the first Industrial Revolution, but from the first Industrial Revolution onwards a core aim for most countries has been to industrialize following the principles of capital accumulation, productivity growth, and output expansion, requiring an ever-increasing amount of energy and resources. Technological advancement and mechanization were huge enablers of this, as was the system of capitalism, bringing hordes of people into wage labour and incentivizing owners of capital to constantly bring in more profit and expand output. As more and more countries have industrialized, global resource use and greenhouse gas emissions have dramatically increased. In the late 1990s, the world passed the threshold for sustainable material footprint. Now, we are about to surpass the threshold for sustainable material footprint if we had resources equivalent to two planets.

If we accept that countries in the global South need to industrialize in order to develop their economies, we face a big problem: it does not seem like it is ecologically sustainable. In this chapter, I have been searching for solutions to this problem but also for trade-offs we ultimately have to face. Green paradigms such as green growth, Green New Deals, and green industrial policy offer useful solutions to meeting the challenge of ecological breakdown, especially outlining practical ways and policy solutions to increase clean and renewable energy supply. They also offer great insights into how we can steer innovation in industrial production to accomplish a green transition. But the green paradigms do not sufficiently address the challenge of how we can deal with the rapid and unsustainable growth in demand—for energy, surely, but especially for the earth's resources—that show no signs of slowing down. To deal with these issues, we have to take a closer look at solutions that call for systemic change.

The degrowth perspective offers useful insights in this respect. Degrowth calls for a drastic reduction in global energy and resource use. At the heart of this strategy is a transition towards a post-capitalist world. Degrowth sees capitalism as the main culprit behind excess energy and resource use because the never-ending search for more profit and capital accumulation—with disregard for ecological sustainability—is a fundamental part of the capitalist system. Some solutions offered by degrowth are, of course, radical, but many are, in fact, practically feasible to implement within a capitalist system. For example, degrowth pushes hard for reclaiming the commons, calling for an end to the for-profit organization of the economy in areas such as housing, utilities, transportation, land, finance, and health. These are all areas that actually used to be part of the commons before they became subject to a massive privatization drive starting in the 1980s. Degrowth also calls for forcefully scaling down ecologically damaging activities, for instance, advertising, planned obsolescence in industrial production, industrial agriculture, and ecologically damaging consumption by the rich. Simple fixes can go a long way in achieving progress here, including tighter regulations in advertising (we already regulate where, what, and how companies can advertise), longer warranties on manufactured goods, actively scaling down the beef industry (the beef industry takes up far more land than any other agricultural activity), and luxury taxes on private jets and yachts.

Where does this leave us with industrialization and industrial policy in the global South? Remember that degrowth calls for a reduction in energy and resource use in high-income countries—and specifically, among wealthy people in those countries—not in the global South. The reason for this is that high-income countries are the ones causing ecological breakdown and are also the ones responsible for ecological breakdown in the near and distant past. Although degrowth leaves the question of development and industrialization in the global South somewhat unanswered, the implication of the evidence on ecological breakdown is clear: countries in the global South should have more leeway to implement policies that leave a material footprint. In other words, these countries should have more 'ecological policy space'. There is also a case to be made for more ecological policy space in the global South, seeing that GDP growth has decreasing marginal utility—GDP growth has a much bigger impact on poverty reduction and development in low-income than in high-income countries. That being said, countries in the global South should, of course, embrace and look for ecologically sustainable ways to industrialize. But this is a gradual process. As I have underscored in this chapter, the process of technological development and innovation for a green economy is a process of building up advanced capabilities in manufacturing. It is unrealistic to expect countries in the global South to implement green industrial policies prior to building up any advanced manufacturing capabilities. Rather, we should expect green industrial policy be phased in alongside industrialization.

In our quest to reverse ecological breakdown while, at the same time, supporting industrialization in the global South, we surely face challenges and trade-offs. Reducing energy and resource use in high-income countries does not come without practical and political hurdles. And if we do achieve degrowth in the global North, this might slow down the prospect for export-oriented industrialization in the global South, which is what characterized the most successful cases of industrialization in the twentieth century. But the epic proportions of ecological breakdown we are witnessing now are unparalleled in human history. We are bound to face uncomfortable challenges and trade-offs. Development and industrialization models for the twenty-first century, without doubt, will have to look different.

6

Industrial policy for the future

So far in this book, I have mostly discussed how megatrends are (or aren't) changing the nature of industrialization.[1] I have yet to answer the 'So what?' question—what are the implications for national and international policy, given my preceding analyses? That is what this chapter is about. The first element of the answer to the 'So what?' question revolves explicitly around industrial policy. More specifically, I offer ideas for national policymakers to achieve industrialization, innovation, and, more broadly, economic development that take into account the four megatrends I have discusses in the book. But, as my analysis thus far in the book has revealed, national policy is not enough: we also need to step into the realm of global governance and international policy to level the playing field in the global economy. This is why the second element of the answer to the 'So what?' question focuses on international efforts to create a global economy that works to serve all countries within it rather than just a few. This second element is, however, related to industrial policy in many ways because I focus on reforms that will allow developing countries the 'policy space' to upgrade their industrial structures. In this sense, industrial policy is a recurring theme throughout the chapter.

The chapter is organized around six policy pillars. They are 'pillars' in the sense that they form only a foundation for reforming and designing policy—they are not a blueprint, tailored to the specific needs and conditions of a country. The sequence of the six policy pillars roughly follows the sequence of the megatrends in the book, meaning that I start out with policy pillars that have to do with the direct technological impact on industrialization (e.g. the rise of services and digital automation technologies) before turning to policy

The Future of the Factory. Jostein Hauge, Oxford University Press. © Jostein Hauge (2023).
DOI: 10.1093/oso/9780198861584.003.0007

pillars more relevant to international political economy and ecology (e.g. the globalization of production and ecological breakdown). But this does not mean that each policy pillar builds on the former ones. The policy pillars can be read independently and in whichever order one would like.

Policy pillar no. 1: Traditional industrial policy still has a role to play

The world economy is constantly changing. Accordingly, we should change our solutions and propositions to tackle pressing economic issues and problems. We cannot be stuck in the past, rehashing policy propositions and insights from 20, 50, 100, or 200 years ago. But it is crucial to understand the distinction between history that holds lessons for the present and history that does not hold lessons for the present. Admittedly, we do not always do a bad job of carrying on insights from the distant past that have relevance for the present. David Ricardo's theory of comparative advantage is still useful to understand the benefits of international trade, of which today's textbooks in economics remind us. Karl Marx's writings on class conflict are as relevant now as they ever were—writings that continue to have a profound impact in shaping modern social science.

However, on the matter of industrial policy, we are sometimes too quick to dismiss lessons from the past. Trade-oriented industrial policy is a good case in point. The economist, Richard Baldwin, says that countries' approaches to industrial policy needs to be updated because 'Before 1985, successful industrialization meant building a domestic supply chain. Today, industrialisers join supply chains and grow rapidly because offshored production brings elements that took Korea and Taiwan decades to develop domestically.' [2] In some ways, he is right in saying that we need to update our industrial policy toolkit, but in other ways, he is mistaken. There are still many useful lessons to learn from industrial policy in South Korea and Taiwan in the second half of the twentieth century (Baldwin's example). One lesson is the manner in which South Korea and Taiwan carefully balanced the need for industrial policy to push for exports (export-oriented industrialization) while, at the same time, protecting certain domestic industries (import substitution industrialization). A second lesson is how South Korea and Taiwan linked up to the strategies of US-based transnational corporations, by manufacturing products for them, but cleverly transferred technology and know-how from these corporations to the domestic economy. This was achieved by means of many policy instruments, an important one being heavy bargaining with the US-based corporations on matters such as local content shares in production and local ownership shares in joint ventures.[3] This second lesson holds a lot of value for industrial policy in today's developing countries because cross-border investments and trade in intermediate goods have skyrocketed.

The reason I discuss the cases of South Korea and Taiwan, other than these being Baldwin's examples, is because they are the two most successful cases of catch-up industrialization during a time when the world economy was somewhat different, albeit not too much so. Another reason is that we now have access to a wealth of industrial policy literature on these two countries (an industrial policy bank of sorts), developed since the 1990s, that we should not be too quick to dismiss. I should stress that there is absolutely no guarantee that countries that emulate aspects of industrial policy in South Korean and Taiwan will achieve the same development success. There were a range of other factors influencing the development outcome of these two countries, including the domestic political economy, the geopolitical climate of the time, and geographical factors. But different or unique conditions for industrial policy in South Korea and Taiwan does not imply that there are no useful lessons to learn from these countries.

By focusing on South Korea and Taiwan, I am certainly not saying that there aren't other countries to learn useful lessons from. China, for example, industrialized even later than South Korea and Taiwan, and, in that sense, hold some lessons that are more useful for today's developing countries. But even industrial policy from the distant past hold useful lessons. If we accept that David Ricardo and

Karl Marx are useful for contemporary analysis, why not Alexander Hamilton, a Founding Father not only of the United States but also of the infant industry argument. Alexander Hamilton is so important to remember because he is, in many ways, the evidence that the country we know today as the land of the free market, the United States, caught up technologically with Great Britain in the nineteenth century by doing the opposite, namely, by being a bastion of protectionism. You may recall from Chapter 5 of this book that Hamilton urged the US Congress to raise tariffs on imported products from Great Britain so that his country could more easily nurture and develop its domestic industries (laying the foundation for what has become known as the infant industry argument). Throughout the nineteenth century, the United States had the highest levels of tariffs in the world on manufactured products. Developing countries today should not necessarily raise tariffs to the level of the United States in the nineteenth century, but Hamilton's advice should still resonate among policymakers today because countries that are technologically lagging behind need to use policy tools to nurture and protect their domestic industry in their infancy.

Policy pillar no. 2: Industrial policy should target, but in all sectors of the economy

In order for industrial policy to be successful, it needs to target something that has the potential to add value to the economy— whether it be a firm, a cluster of firms, a state-driven activity, or an entire industry. When I use the words 'add value' I am implying 'value-added', a very important term in economics. At a micro level, value-added describes the economic enhancement a firm gives to its products or services before selling them on to other firms or directly to customers. More value-added within a firm generally means more revenue and profits for that firm. At a macro level, value-added is the market value of the aggregate output of a defined set of economic activities minus the market value of the aggregate inputs that go into that set of economic activities. If all stages of value-added occurred within a country's borders, the total value-added is what is counted in gross domestic product (GDP). The process of adding value often entails productivity growth and innovation. In turn, this is what drives economic development and a transformation of a country's productive structure from less to more advanced.

Why am I getting so technical about this term, 'value-added'? If you read the above paragraph carefully and think about industrial policy in the context of what you are reading, you might understand why: adding value can be achieved in a number of different ways. Think about a company that only assembles phones. If that company starts manufacturing the components of the phone as well as assembling them, it will have achieved value-added in the production process. It will probably achieve even more value-added if it starts engaging in the research and design (R&D), design, and branding/marketing activities of the phone as well. Remember from Chapter 5 how the decomposition of the value-added stages of an iPhone revealed that Apple rakes in more than 50% of the final retail price of the phone despite not making any of the components? It does so by specializing in R&D, design, and branding/marketing activities. Officially, these types of activities are service activities, not manufacturing activities. I am reaching an important point here: industrial policy is largely about targeting activities to achieve higher value-added for the economy as a whole, and achieving so does not limit itself to the traditional manufacturing sector. In fact, at present, many service activities in manufacturing value chains are making up larger shares of value-added than the manufacturing activities themselves. The iPhone value chain is a perfect case in point. This is why well-crafted industrial policy should target both manufacturing and services. But why stop there? Why not also agricultural activities? For example, in a cocoa value chain, the companies that sell the chocolates and the companies that make the cocoa paste earn more revenue and make up larger shares of value-added in the cocoa value chain than the farmers that harvest and dry the cocoa beans.[4]

In both the instances of a phone's value chain and a chocolate's value chain, the boundaries between agriculture, manufacturing, and services are clearly blurred. But a lot of it does boil down to manufacturing. The people who design an iPhone rely on production and engineering knowhow and are integral to the manufacturing process on the factory floor. Making a chocolate bar out of cocoa beans involves transforming raw materials into a finished product through the use of machinery and factory facilities—clearly a manufacturing process at the core. This is why, when you take a step back and look at the aggregate evidence on the difference between high-income and low-income countries, you clearly see that almost all high-income countries have gone through a process of industrialization, involving an expansion of manufacturing output. Even in those countries that have experienced a decline in manufacturing output, including the United States and the United Kingdom, the manufacturing capabilities built up over time are still a core part of those countries' innovation systems.

Ultimately, though, for the purposes of industrial policy, it's not that important to make distinctions between sectors of the economy that clearly have blurred boundaries and are, at times, arbitrarily defined. For the purposes of industrial policy, the most important task is to find and appropriately target those activities that have the highest potential for value-added and, hence, economic development and innovation. But I would still maintain that those activities will often be found in the manufacturing sector or be closely linked to manufacturing processes by shared knowhow, capabilities, and/or the use of inputs.

Policy pillar no. 3: Automation is a challenge (of smaller proportions)

There are growing fears that automation technologies will start displacing jobs at a faster rate than they have in the past, especially in labour-intensive manufacturing. Advances in artificial intelligence are enabling digital systems to perform tasks previously performed by humans. It is believed that this, combined with other technologies associated with the so-called fourth Industrial Revolution (like the miniaturization of computers, increased computing power, and continuous data collection through the internet-of-things) will make it feasible to automate more work across more industries in a short period of time.

In Chapter 4, I analysed the impact of automation on employment in the past and present, as well as in the future, discussing the most granular forecast studies published on the subject. My analysis indicated that predictions of large-scale job displacement are exaggerated. Automation technologies will most likely result in a reorganization of the labour force rather than large-scale job displacement and unemployment, in line with historical trends. The PC created 15.8 million more jobs than it displaced in the United States between 1980 and 2015. A comprehensive study looking at automation's impact on employment across twenty-one Organisation for Economic Co-operation and Development (OECD) countries in the 2010s (2012–19) finds no support for net job destruction. In fact, the study finds that countries facing higher overall automation risk in 2012 experienced higher employment growth over the subsequent period.[5] This is because automation technologies create (as well as destroy) jobs by giving rise to new technologies, new jobs, and new industries and by contributing to productivity growth.

Nonetheless, automation technologies will have a disruptive impact on certain industries, as, indeed, suggested by some forecast studies. The global consultancy firm McKinsey published a report in 2017 estimating that between 75 million and 275 million workers in the world (3–14% of the global workforce) will need to switch occupational categories by 2030.[6] Therefore, countries need to have policies in place to mitigate such disruptions and to smoothly manage the decline of certain industries—or, at least, the decline of the role of human labour in certain industries. Industrial policy has an important role to play, especially in designing policies to facilitate occupational transitions, manage adjustment costs, and more broadly 'reskill' the labour force. The OECD is doing important work in this area. Focusing on its member countries, they have identified possible occupational transitions (i.e. workers that can change jobs) with short retraining periods (up to six months), moderate retraining periods (up to one year), and serious retraining periods (up to three years).[7] Most importantly, they identify occupations that are at high risk of automation which, at the same time, cannot be easily 'reskilled' (in other words, occupations that require the longest retraining periods). These include blacksmiths, mining and construction workers, subsistence farmers in the livestock industry, and various machine operators in rubber, plastics, metal, and mineral processing plants. This kind of work by the OECD is exactly the kind of work that will help governments to more easily mitigate the disruptions caused by automation technologies.

When we talk about overcoming the automation challenge, it is important to stress that this is not a challenge of equal proportions all over the world. In the global South, less than 5% of manufacturing firms use advanced digital production technologies, and in some countries, over 70% of manufacturing firms only use analogue production technologies.[8] The UN Conference for Trade and Development has criticized existing studies on automation for only investigating technical feasibility of implementation, leaving out the question of economic feasibility of implementation—an incredibly important question in the context of the global South.[9] One could also criticize global forecast models for actually not using global data but rather extrapolating globally based on labour market data in high-income countries. Unless we assume that automation will accelerate reshoring of production from the global South to the global North (which I have indicated earlier in the book is not happening on a large scale), overcoming the automation challenge seems to be mainly a challenge in *some* industries in *some* countries in the global North.

Policy pillar no. 4: Make trade fair, not free

As my analysis in Chapter 5 revealed, the globalization of production and the global governance of trade favours countries and transnational corporations based in the global North. Specialization and export patterns between countries in the global North, on the one hand, and countries in the global South, on the other hand, reflect

an uneven and unfair system of economic exchange. Free, unfet-
tered trade will only reinforce this pattern. Free trade is clearly not
fair trade, and international trade agreements need to reflect this. To
start, agreements within the World Trade Organization (WTO) need
to allow developing countries more policy space—space to regulate
trade so that they can more easily upgrade their industrial structures
and develop their economies. This means relaxing constraints on the
use of direct and indirect trade subsidies, such as tax credits, rent
rebates, and export subsidies. It means possibly removing the protection of intellectual property rights from multilateral trade rules
to make technology more easily accessible to countries in the global
South. It means strengthening antitrust and antimonopoly laws,
which would help to loosen the stranglehold that transnational corporations have over the global economy. Global governance experts,
Kevin Gallagher and Richard Kozul-Wright, suggest that a good
start would be to reintroduce regulatory structures that have been
dismantled over the past forty years, for example, the 'Set of Mul-
tilaterally Agreed Equitable Principles and Rules for the Control
of Restrictive Business Practices' adopted by the United Nations
General Assembly in 1980.[10] Antitrust legislation is also the responsibility of national policymakers in high-income countries. In this
respect, the United States could look to learn from the European
Union in their efforts to curb the dominant position of transnational
corporations in the digital space.

In addition to reforming its rules, the WTO needs to be democra-
tized. On paper, the WTO is democratic, with no one member state
having more voting power than another member state. In practice,
however, high-income countries can afford more and better trade
negotiators and permanent representatives at the WTO headquar-
ters in Geneva. This problem could easily be solved if the WTO
were to set up a common fund to cover costs of negotiators for low-
income and middle-income countries in such a way that all countries have equal punching power at the negotiating table.[11] There is
also a strong case to be made for ditching the investor–state dispute
settlement mechanism in the WTO, which allows transnational corporations to sue sovereign states for regulations that compromise

their profits. Disputes in a multilateral trading system should be settled state-to-state through national court systems, which are more transparent, public, and accountable.

We need more fair trade not only for countries in the global South but also for workers in the global South. Workers at the bottom rung of global value chains get little more than pennies for toiling endless hours on the factory floor. This is even the case in China, a country whose firms have, in many ways, successfully integrated into global value chains. How can we improve the working conditions and wages of workers in the global South? Historically, the most effective way to ensure better conditions for workers has been to allow workers to organize themselves and to form a collective voice, for example through trade unions. Unfortunately, not all workers in all countries are granted the freedom to organize. It is not just the state that is to blame here—transnational corporations also drive a race to the bottom in labour standards by demanding low wages in countries to which they offshore production. Luckily, in some instances, there are incentives for both states and corporations to improve labour standards. I presented research from Ethiopia earlier in the book, showing how low wages can lead to turnover rates so high that it reduces the profits of firms. Satisfied workers can clearly lead to better results at the firm level.

However, legislation at the national level is not enough in a world of globalized production. Seeing that capital has become incredibly mobile, we also need global coordination to improve labour standards. In this respect, an interesting proposition is gaining momentum: set a global minimum wage pegged to decent living standards in each country.[12] Some experts claim that the International Labour Organization has the will and capacity to govern a global minimum wage system. But the problem with the International Labour Organization is that it represents states and businesses as well as workers, which means that a proposition of a global minimum wage will be controversial within the organization. Because of this, we might need to push for an international agreement on a global minimum wage within the UN General Assembly. This has actually been done successfully on a similar issue, namely, the Universal Declaration of

Human Rights, drafted by representatives from all over the world and proclaimed by the United Nations (UN) General Assembly in 1948.

Not all solutions are to be found through reforms within current organizations and structures. Sometimes, we need to look to new structures. On the trade front, some notable alternatives to the WTO are, in fact, emerging, which could serve countries in the global South better than the WTO. For example, the Regional Comprehensive Economic Partnership (RCEP) signed by Asia-Pacific nations in 2020 has become the largest trade bloc in history. The African Continental Free Trade Area (AfCFTA) is another massive trade area, recently created by fifty-four of the fifty-five African Union nations. These trade agreements may not be a magic bullet for all countries that take part in them, but generally, regional and bilateral trade agreements between countries of similar income levels are more beneficial for low-income and middle-income countries compared to the WTO framework, where these countries get overpowered by high-income countries.

Reforming, reorganizing, and rethinking the system of global governance is one of the most important steps towards a more equitable system of international trade. But even in the current system of hyperglobalization and globalized production dominated by transnational corporations based in the global North, not all hope is lost. We should not lose sight of the ability that governments in the global South have to determine their own fate, strategically utilizing international trade networks and global value chains for their own economic development. China, although not a fairy-tale success story in all aspects, is a great example of a country that has done just that. Since the 1980s, China has massively ramped up its participation in global value chains through the attraction of foreign investment and the establishment of special economic zones. The country linked up to transnational corporations based in the global North, identifying niche industrial activities that added value and employment, using this as a springboard for further industrialization. Between 2000 and 2008, a time when China's economic growth rate was at peak levels, the country accounted for more than two-thirds of the world's exports in processed goods.[13] Today, China has successfully launched its own global brands and taken a lead role in some global value chains. Huawei, the Chinese multinational technology corporation, is the prime example.

There is, of course, a reason that China has had more success with participation in global value chains than many other developing countries. China bargained heavily with foreign investors, often insisting on joint ownership with foreign firms as a way of transferring technology and know-how from foreign firms to the domestic economy and as a way of having more control over the operations of these foreign firms in China. The manner in which the state oversaw these joint ventures was often through the use of state-owned enterprises—the state itself frequently went into joint business ventures with foreign firms. Today, more than 50,000 firms in China are partly or fully owned by the state. This is by far the largest number of state-owned enterprises in any country.[14]

State-owned enterprises have been important for economic development in many other countries too. The reason is simple: they help to maintain national security, economic autonomy from multinational capital, and control over strategic industries and national resources. Another important rationale for using state-owned enterprises in economic development policy is that the government has the best ability to take on investment projects that are too risky for the private sector. The state-owned enterprises set up this way are not necessarily linked to foreign capital, they 'circumvent' foreign capital; that is, they are investment projects completely designed for and by the domestic economy. The South Korean steel company, POSCO, is a great example, set up in 1968 as a state-owned enterprise. POSCO was ridiculed by the World Bank when it was first introduced because South Korea had no capabilities in steel production in the 1960s. It was clearly an incredibly risky venture. Today, POSCO is the fourth largest steel producer in the world. The example of POSCO goes to show that industrial policy needs to avoid and circumvent transnational capital in addition to linking up to it in order to be truly successful. State-owned enterprises are surely risky endeavours and hold no guarantee of success, but development strategies in the global South that rely completely on linking up to the agendas of transnational corporations from higher-income countries have zero chance of success.

Policy pillar no. 5: The case for ecological policy space

We are living in an age of ecological breakdown, and it is posing a challenge to industrialization. How? Global warming and unsustainable resource use are directly related to economic growth, productivity growth, capital accumulation, and therefore, by extension, industrialization. On a global scale, we only started witnessing explosive growth rates in output, greenhouse gas emissions, and resource use after the onset of the first Industrial Revolution in the late eighteenth century. It is no coincidence that climate scientists use temperatures at 'pre-industrial levels' as a benchmark to gauge global warming today.

Technological advancements in industrial production have been huge enablers of ecological breakdown, but luckily, they also hold some promise as a solution. In fact, they have already proven themselves as such. Think about wind turbines, photovoltaic cells (solar panels), nuclear power plants, hydroelectric dams, and electric vehicles. These are innovations that have helped us and continue to help us move towards clean and renewable energy use. Clearly, industrial policy (more specifically, green industrial policy) has a role to play in saving our planet. At the most obvious level, it plays a role in steering us towards policy and investment decisions that encourage sustainable economic development. Unless incentivized by the state, the free market has not exactly proven itself as an ardent supporter of investments in new and renewed energy systems, energy infrastructure, or energy efficiency. We have already seen how green industrial policy has been able to steer the market towards sustainability through things like carbon taxes, feed-in tariffs (long-term government contracts that provide above-market prices for renewable energy producers), R&D support for renewable energy, subsidized credit, and public procurement. Research on green industrial policy is also doing a good job at suggesting how we can fund and steer large-scale public projects to achieve global net-zero emissions as fast as possible.[15]

But green industrial policy is not enough. At least not in the way that green industrial policy has been pitched in recent years, which is a policy or a set of policies to steer the economy towards net-zero emissions by greening *supply* of energy. This traditional way of thinking about green industrial policy does not sufficiently address the challenge of how we can deal with the rapid and unsustainable growth in *demand* for energy and for the earth's resources, both of which show no signs of slowing down. In fact, the countries that have made the most progress in green innovation and implemented the 'greenest' industrial policies (by and large today's high-income countries) are the ones most rapidly depleting the earth's resources and contributing the most to global warming. High-income countries are running their economies way more unsustainably than low-income countries. According to an article published in *Lancet Planet Health*, low-income countries and lower-middle-income countries combined were responsible for a mere 1% of global excess resource use between 1970 and 2017.[16] What is going on here? It's simple: it's excessive growth. It is therefore urgent that we talk about policies that tackle unsustainable ways of living head on.

Clearly, countries around the world do not share equal blame for ecological breakdown. This is where 'ecological policy space' comes in. The idea of ecological policy space is that countries that have contributed less (and are contributing less) to ecological breakdown should have more space to implement industrial policy as they see fit, with less concern for energy and resource use. The case for ecological policy space is a call for high-income countries to urgently put their own house in order before preaching sustainability to countries in the global South. In what world should it be okay to push green industrial policy onto countries that are responsible for less than 1% of global excess resource use? The global North has colonized the planet's ecological commons,[17] and the number one priority should be to decolonize it.

The pressing need for decolonization of our ecological commons is not the only argument in favour of more ecological policy space for countries in the global South. A second argument is that economic growth (i.e. growth in output and material use) is a more urgent need for countries in the global South because people at lower levels of income more urgently need growth in order to live better and healthier lives. If any countries should be allowed to pursue growth by whichever means, it should be countries in the global South. A third argument is that capabilities in sustainable industrial production do not appear magically out of thin air—it is a step-by-step process involving years of developing capabilities in the industrial sector more broadly, often starting out with cheaper and 'dirtier' sectors with lower entry barriers. Why do you think we see more electric vehicles, LED light bulbs, and high-tech waste management systems in high-income countries? Of course, you will find impressive green industrial capabilities developed in middle-income countries such as Brazil, China, and India, in, for example, hydropower and wind turbines. But building up these capabilities has been a gradual process that often started with a less ecologically sustainable path. It is unrealistic to assume that low-income countries will be able to manufacture and scale up green technologies as rapidly as high-income countries have done.

Of course, this is not to say that there is no merit to traditional green industrial policy in the global South. All countries in the world should look to be making green transitions, targeting and supporting industries that have the potential to save our planet, while, at the same time, scaling down industries that are destroying our planet. But the responsibility to change the status quo of our destructive path should lie with the countries that have led us onto this path. Therefore, the discussion on ecological policy space should be about how we can increase this space for countries in the global South. In turn, this discussion should be about decreasing energy and resource use in the global North. The traditional green industrial policies, overly focused on scaling up the supply of clean and renewable energy, have proved inadequate.

One channel of pushing countries in the global North to scale down excess energy and resource use is through international pressure. Unfortunately, we have made little progress on this front. A big obstacle is that the countries that are causing ecological breakdown suffer disproportionately less from it because they have the money, power, and technology to mitigate many of the negative effects. And it doesn't help that the world economy is essentially a structure in which sovereign states compete against one another, cooperating only when it serves them. This is why it's so difficult to achieve meaningful cooperation on climate action and ecological matters. The Paris Agreement adopted in 2015 was a good step in the right direction, but, like most other international climate initiatives, it has been mostly talk with no action. In fact, over two dozen UN climate change conferences have taken place over the past thirty years. Given the continued growth in excess resource use and greenhouse gas emissions during this time period, these conferences have essentially done nothing to reverse ecological breakdown. Most scientists have, by now, concluded that reducing greenhouse gas emissions by 50% by 2030—a core aim of the Paris Agreement—is an illusion.

It is probably a better bet that countries take action based on domestic rather than international pressure. Fortunately, green parties are rising everywhere, and green policies are becoming more prominent on political and policy agendas around the world. On the domestic front, four policy interventions in high-income countries can help to increase the ecological policy space in low- and middle-income countries. First, high-income countries need to identify the most ecologically destructive industries and start scaling them down—focusing on consumption in their own countries and, by consequence, related production in other countries. Some of these industries cut across many sectors of the economy, including the advertising industry and the oil industry, but others are much more specific, for example, the beef industry. Second, we need to target and scale down the wasteful and useless consumption habits of millionaires and billionaires as they account for a disproportionately large share of energy and resource use. Taxes on environmentally harmful luxury products, such as private jets and superyachts, is a good place to start. Third, energy and resource use in industrial production would considerably decrease if we started incentivizing the manufacture of long-lasting products. Ending our culture of planned obsolescence is not that hard: if, say, manufacturers in the electronics industry were held to guarantees of at least ten years, we would see many more long-lasting products. Fourth, high-income countries need to shift from individual to community-centred living. More public transport is the most important area, but our material footprint and our energy use would improve if we shared more land, housing, and recreational areas. This is not some far-fetched dream that is unachievable in our current economic system. High-income countries that have moved away from community-centred living simply have to start reversing the mass privatization of public goods and services that has taken place over the past decades.

Many of the abovementioned policy interventions should, of course, also be considered by low-income and middle-income countries—for example, overconsumption by billionaires and soil degradation caused by the beef industry are global problems. However, the point is that these interventions are most urgently needed in the countries that are overshooting their fair share of energy and resource use.

Policy pillar no. 6: Do not lose sight of the systemic change needed

Events in the past few years have rattled the world economy in unprecedented ways. The COVID-19 pandemic has not only been a health crisis but also an economic crisis, causing an abrupt stop to many economic activities and disruptions to international trade. Talk of deglobalization, reshoring, and regionalization of supply chains hit a high when the pandemic exposed the fragility of our interconnected world. The war in Ukraine has been a wakeup call in similar ways. Physical blockades and the destruction of productive capacity in Ukraine, on the one hand, and economic sanctions on Russia, on the other hand, raised the global price of commodities of which Russia and Ukraine are key exporters, such as oil, natural gas, wheat, barley, pig iron, and fertilizer.[18] The impact was especially painful for countries directly dependent on imports from either Russia or Ukraine—particularly those countries trying to phase out imports from Russia as part of economic sanctions. Many countries in the world also reduced or banned their exports of wheat due to an acute shortage of it.

Globalization has clearly been put to the test these past few years. We will surely see a different kind of globalization in the future as some countries will look to secure stronger domestic or regional access to some inputs in some industries. However, as I pointed out in both Chapters 4 and 5, globalization has, in many ways, bounced back and is still going strong. Reshoring is accelerating but on a much smaller scale than continued offshoring, and manufacturers in high-income countries say that they will continue to import inputs from across the globe in the future. A close look at trade metrics suggests that globalization is, in fact, back on track, right where it was before the pandemic: in absolute numbers, levels of global economic output, global trade, and global foreign direct investments have all surpassed pre-pandemic levels.

What am I trying to say with all of this? I'm trying to say that we need to be cautiously sceptical of the news hype that the world is changing. With respect to globalization, specifically, it is important to understand the ways in which the COVID-19 pandemic and the war in Ukraine has changed, and is changing, globalization, international trade, and supply chains. But it is more important to identify and talk about solutions to the structural and systemic issues in the current era of globalization—issues that have continued during these events but that these events have unfortunately overshadowed. Globalization in its post-1980s form is still alive and kicking: a type of globalization that has exacerbated uneven and unfair economic exchange between the global South and the global North, benefiting the latter at the expense of the former.

More than ever, it is important not to lose sight of the systemic inequalities between the global South and the global North. The pandemic started some discussions among high-income countries about how they could use the fall in economic activity and output as an opportunity to rebuild their economies in an ecologically sustainable way. There was some hope that high-income countries would start to take their fair share of the blame in causing ecological breakdown, but these discussions were eventually overshadowed by the need to get economic growth back on track. And it didn't help that inflation and the fear of recession started to loom in high-income countries in the wake of the war in Ukraine.

In short, there are two developments that should concern us more than anything: (i) in absolute terms, incomes between the global South and the global North have steadily been diverging for more than fifty years; (ii) ecological breakdown has been caused, and continues to be caused, by countries in the global North. These facts are caused by systemic imbalances in the world economy that I have outlined in this book, and, in this chapter, I have tried to offer some solutions for systemic change. But in order for systemic change to happen, these issues need to occupy a greater space in public discourse. We therefore need to work against the news cycle overshadowing the most important systemic issues of our time.

Conclusion

A factory in the future

Mechanized production and the factory system have shaped the modern world and modern capitalism. The Industrial Revolution in the late eighteenth century enabled Great Britain and a few other Northern powers to separate themselves economically and technologically from the rest of the world. By the twentieth century, industrialization had come to be seen as the driver of economic growth, development, and innovation. It also became a tool for military expansion, imperialism, and for securing an edge in international trade. We eventually saw the rise of two distinct groups of countries in the world: one was rich and industrialized, the other was poor and dependent on agriculture and natural resources. 'Industrialized' countries and 'developed' countries came to be seen as two sides of the same coin.

In the future, will industrialization and factory-based production keep remaking and reshaping the world? Will automation technologies make human work in factories completely redundant? Will factories continue to make ever smaller inputs and parts of final products, spread across the world to form complex value chains and production networks? Or perhaps the number of factories will start dwindling altogether, dwarfed by the expansion of the service economy? What will future factories look like, considering the harmful ecological impact of industrialization? These are some of the key questions I have tackled throughout the book. Now, let me summarize my answers but, specifically, with 'a factory in the future' in mind.

The Future of the Factory. Jostein Hauge, Oxford University Press. © Jostein Hauge (2023).
DOI: 10.1093/oso/9780198861584.003.0008

The rise of services

Will workers at a factory in the future be absent from the factory floor and rather be engaged in service work? In many ways, this is already the case. But workers sitting on a computer rather than being on the factory floor are not necessarily disengaged from the manufacturing process. They might be designing a product or be involved in research and development (R&D) activities, all of which often require engineering know-how. Is it correct to categorize such activities as services rather than manufacturing? In Chapter 2, my answer to this question was a cautious no. The manufacturing sector is still more integral to the economy than our national accounts indicate. We might have fewer factories today (and most likely in the future) compared to the past, but today, people do not have to physically be at a factory in order to take part in the manufacturing process. Admittedly, many services in today's economies don't have anything to do with manufacturing. However, manufacturing and factory-based production are important to a host of services, also those who do not rely directly on manufacturing know-how. The most productive and innovative services are highly dependent on manufactured products, for instance, hardware chips, information transmission technologies, fibre optics, and satellites, to name a few. Even if we accept that the economic contribution of manufacturing is counted accurately in countries' national accounts, which will reveal that the manufacturing sector contributes less to economic output today than in the past, there is still good reason to question the claim that the world economy has experienced massive de-industrialization. If we look more closely at the data on global manufacturing, we will see that a lot of manufacturing has simply relocated to a small number of countries in East Asia, particularly China, rather than diminished everywhere.

While I remain firm in my belief that the manufacturing sector will play a vital part in future development and growth strategies, we should not ignore or underestimate the growing ability of services—especially digital ones—to contribute to productivity growth, international trade, and economic development. Some of today's largest global technology companies, including Amazon, Google, or Meta, hardly manufacture things. And while these companies might be tied more closely to the wealth of high-income countries, we are also seeing low-income and middle-income countries reaping some economic benefits from services, such as India, Kenya, the Philippines, and Rwanda.

Digital automation technologies

Will production processes at a factory in the future become more automated, displacing workers in the process? Yes, it is highly likely that automation technologies will displace tasks performed by humans, but let's keep in mind that automation-induced job displacement is not a new phenomenon. We can, in fact, trace it back more than 200 years to the Luddite protests in Nottingham, when textile artisans and weavers protested the use of automation technologies in textile factories. More recently, we have seen digital technologies (e.g. the personal computer, PC) displace tasks performed by humans. Throughout history, both in the near and distant past, the introduction of new technologies has undoubtedly disrupted labour markets, but they have not resulted in large-scale job displacement. The reason for this is that automation technologies create as well as displace jobs, as I reiterated in Chapter 3. They do so through improving productivity both at the firm level and the economy level and by creating demand for new jobs that didn't exist before.

There are, however, rumblings that this time around, and in the future, things will look different due to the introduction of artificial intelligence (AI)-related technologies. We are now seeing the emergence of technologies and products that not only manually act like humans but also think like humans. Think about the massively popular chatbot, ChatGPT, which can answer almost any question you throw at it with impressive clarity and intellectual depth. But we should be cautiously sceptical of the hype surrounding AI. The most granular studies looking at the future impact of automation technologies predict labour reorganization in line with historical trends rather than large-scale job displacement. We actually have some evidence already with respect to automation's impact on jobs in the AI era. A paper entitled, 'What Happened to Jobs at High Risk of Automation?' finds that those countries facing higher overall automation risk in the early 2010s experienced *higher* employment growth than other countries in subsequent years.

We also need to be sceptical of the AI hype from a scale-up perspective. For decades, there has been a tendency to hype up the expected impact of new technologies on social and economic organization. Did the 1930s prediction of flying cars play out? No. AI is still just a small fraction of the entire market for information and communication technology. In the global South, the implementation of digital technologies in production is lagging far behind the global North. Some people are making the case that this doesn't matter because automated factories in the global North will 'reshore' jobs from the global South. Evidence indicates otherwise. Reshoring is still happening at a smaller scale than continued offshoring, and the most high-profile case of reshoring—Adidas's automated speedfactories in Germany and the United States—failed miserably.

Globalization of production

The topic of reshoring is a good segway into a discussion on globalization. In the context of globalized production, where will future factories be located, which factories produce what, and who are the winners and losers? As we saw in Chapter 4, the globalization of production has enabled many more countries, firms, and workers to participate in the global economy. This is especially true for countries in the global South, who, on aggregate, have increased their share of world trade remarkably from the 1980s onwards. Countries can now become internationally competitive in global industries by specializing in niche segments of global value chains rather than making a product from scratch. Some countries in the global South have experienced considerable success through participating in the global economy in this manner. The prime example is China, a country that has found a way to become an integral part of more or less every global industry, becoming the 'world's factory' in the process.

The gains from participating in global value chains are not, however, equal. Quite often, the firms making the actual stuff—the real factories—are losing out. Increasingly, profits and value-added go to the firms specializing in intangible activities in global value chains, such as R&D, marketing, and retail. I showed how Apple takes home more than 50% of the final retail price of an iPhone, despite not making or putting together any of the phone's components. An important reason for this is that the era of globalization we are living in has enabled large transnational corporations, mostly based in the global North, to increase their global reach and power. This enables these corporations to appropriate increasing shares of profits over a larger market. This appropriation of profits is fortified by technological dominance, privileged access to low-cost capital and labour all over the world, low trade barriers, and strong protection of intellectual property. The low trade barriers and the strong protection of intellectual property is, by and large, maintained by rules governing international trade, including the framework of rules within the World Trade Organization (WTO).

In some ways, the globalization of production entered a new era when the COVID-19 pandemic and Russia's invasion of Ukraine exposed the fragility of global interconnectedness. Many pundits now claim that we will see a wave of deglobalization and that more factories in the future will be domestic rather than global. However, while some supply chains have, and will be, reconfigured, global trade has, on aggregate, bounced back, even surpassing pre-pandemic levels. It's not an exaggeration to say that globalization is back on track, and it's important not to let this wave of supply-chain disruptions distract us from the overarching systemic issue in today's era of globalization: a global economy dominated by a few, large, transnational corporations, often raking in profits at the expense of economic development in the global South.

Ecological breakdown

Factories in the future will undoubtedly produce things that are more environmentally friendly and do so in a way that is more ecologically sustainable. This is already happening—from photovoltaic cells and electric vehicles to water filtration systems and bioreactors, the manufacturing sector is a key player in the green transition. But is the green transition keeping up with ever-increasing consumption? It does not look like it. In Chapter 5, I presented the evidence, showing how the share of fossil fuels in final energy demand has stayed firmly at 80% in the 2010s, despite all our efforts to increase the supply of clean and renewable energy in this decade. We are failing more miserably with respect to resource use. Our global material footprint—calculated by adding up the extraction (and, by extension, destruction) of our earth's resources, including biomass, fossil fuels, metal ores, and non-metal ores—has skyrocketed since the mid-twentieth century. And it shows no sign of slowing down. Ironically, even the green energy transition is dependent on the overuse of our earth's resources, including rare-earth metals like lithium and cobalt.

Green paradigms, including green growth, Green New Deals, and green industrial policy, have an important role to play in moving our economies onto a sustainable path. However, they are failing to address the overuse of our earth's resources. This is where degrowth comes in, an emerging paradigm that advocates for a planned reduction in energy and resource use. Degrowth policies are, in some ways, antithetical to capitalism and therefore practically challenging to implement, but there are policy pathways where degrowth and green paradigms meet. For example, in our current economic system, it is not unfeasible to target and scale down the most ecologically destructive industries, target and scale down wasteless consumption habits of wealthy people, incentivize the manufacture of long-lasting products, and reorganize our economies from individual-centred living towards community-centred living.

We see, then, that future factories not only have to become green but also have to make things that last longer, in some cases make less of it (like vehicles for private use), and in extreme cases shut down completely (do we really need any private jets or superyachts?). I need to underscore that responsibility for ecological breakdown is not distributed evenly around the world. Today's high-income countries, and especially wealthy people in high-income countries, are the ones who have got us into this mess. Therefore, these countries need to get their house in order more urgently than anyone else. In this sense, countries in the global South should be granted more 'ecological policy space' when designing their industrial policies and embarking on industrialization strategies.

Levelling the global playing field

Drawing together the analysis of the entire book, what can we say about the future of the factory? An important point I have rehashed throughout the book is that in a world of technological change and technological disruptions, industrialization and factory-based production remains a cornerstone of economic progress. The other point I have rehashed throughout the book is that we need to pay more attention to power and politics in the world economy in order to understand the future of industrialization. Industrialization is a competitive game that involves power, politics, dirty play, and even warfare. It involves firms and sovereign states competing against one another to gain a competitive edge economically, militarily, and technologically. In any competitive game that has no clear end, players not only strategize to get to the top of the podium but also strategize at how power can be wielded to stay on top of the podium once they get there. A few select countries in the global North climbed to the top of the podium during the period of European colonization of the world between the sixteenth and twentieth centuries. This type of colonization no longer exists, but countries in the global North still wield the power they've amassed in any way they can to stay on top of the podium.

The game that is being played now is, in many ways, dirtier and more dishonest than it was during the age of colonization between the sixteenth and twentieth centuries. How? Because we are being told that globalization helps to eliminate poverty in the global South. We are being told that international trade agreements work in favour of countries in the global South. We are being told that we should celebrate international climate agreements even when they don't reflect who is actually responsible for ecological breakdown. In reality, the current system of globalization and international trade vastly favours transnational corporations based in the global North. In reality, a few select countries in the global North are the ones mostly responsible for ecological breakdown. In reality, firms and countries in the global North wield their power in international organizations and through international agreements so that, behind the scenes, these organizations and agreements work in their interests.

The future of the factory and, especially, the future of industrialization in the global South (home to roughly 80% of the world's population) will be determined by how we deal with these power asymmetries in the world economy. Countries in the global South certainly have the autonomy and ability to successfully implement industrial policies in the current global environment, but we also need to work on reforms that reflect a recognition of global power asymmetries and an unlevel playing field. Specifically, reforms and agreements need to reflect that countries in the global South should be allowed more policy space in the arena of international trade—due the current system of uneven economic exchange—and more ecological policy space—reflecting the fact that high-income countries are the ones largely responsible for ecological breakdown.

Additional megatrends and related research directions

I am firm in my belief that the megatrends I have discusses and analysed in this book are the most central to the debate on the changing nature of economic development and industrialization. However, this does not mean that we are not witnessing other shifts and developments in the world economy that are central to this debate. One could also make a case for framing the megatrends differently than I have done, shedding more light on some issues that I have only discussed briefly.

A shift in global economic power is arguably a megatrend in itself.[1] Earlier in the book, I highlighted how the global South's share of world trade and world economic output is increasing. This is not happening everywhere though—China is mainly driving this surge. The emergence of China as a global economic powerhouse has important ramifications for global value chains and industrialization pathways. For one, it will probably result in a restructuring of trade flows and global value chains. This has already happened to some degree, but China will likely become an even more important player in producing various inputs and components in global value chains. Given the country's size and economic power, Chinese firms may also be able to change their positions in global value chains, replacing some lead firms traditionally based in the global North. This is notoriously difficult, as I have rehashed throughout this book, but if one developing country is on a path to challenging the economic hegemony of the global North, it is China.

Given the growth of China's domestic economy and the emergence of a massive middle class in the country, it will also become a more important end market for exports. We may see the emergence of regional value chains in East Asia more prominently, whereby countries of lower income in the region, including Cambodia, Indonesia, Laos, the Philippines, Thailand, and Vietnam, reap benefits from strengthening trade ties with China and serving a growing consumer market in China. It is also possible that other low- and middle-income countries around the world strengthen their trade ties to China. In Africa, China is already the most important trading partner for a majority of countries.

The rise of China in the global economy has also fuelled geopolitical tensions and trade wars. Specifically, it's worth monitoring the relationship between China and the United States. Some would say that tensions between these two countries are rooted in political and ideological differences, but we shouldn't underestimate the economic dimension. Anti-China rhetoric across the political spectrum in the United States and cross-partisan consensus for manufacturing subsidies and protectionist measures only started to become commonplace after the United States realized how dependent—and therefore vulnerable—the US economy had become on imports from China. The COVID-19 pandemic and lockdowns in China also played a role as they exposed the fragility of the strong economic ties between China and the United States.

In Chapter 3, I addressed digital automation technologies as a megatrend, specifically looking at its impact on job displacement. Some would say that the current wave of digital technologies (the so-called fourth Industrial Revolution) deserves a broader analytical scope than I have provided, seeing that these technologies are having a profound impact beyond automation and job displacement. The technologies that are starting to have a larger socio-economic impact—in addition to automation technologies and AI-related technologies—include the internet-of-things (IoT), cloud technologies, big data analytics, and blockchain technologies. According to the UN Industrial Development Organization, many of these new digital technologies are changing the way industrial systems operate and are opening new avenues for productivity growth.[2]

The fourth Industrial Revolution also calls for discussions on the possibility of a widening technological gap between the global South and the global North. One mechanism through which this gap is increasing is simple: high-income countries have more high-tech capabilities in place so the current technological revolution—which is mainly taking place in high-income countries—is shrinking the ability of low- and middle-income countries to be technologically competitive. Another mechanism through which this gap is increasing is through digital platform powers. Certain corporations based in the global North (for instance, Google, Amazon, Facebook, and Microsoft) have amassed immense global power through launching digital platforms that provide services within data infrastructure, data collection, data storage, business operations, and IT systems.[3] If these platforms continue to be characterized by monopoly and oligopoly structures, this will pose a challenge for low-income and middle-income countries who are looking to build local digital platforms. These platforms also provide unprecedented opportunities for a small number of transnational corporations to predict and control people's behaviour due to the vast increase in the amount of data they are able to collect from us.[4] In future years, data will become an immensely important source of power in economic governance.

Predicting the future is a thankless task, almost impossible in the socio-economic realm due to the unpredictable nature of social and economic change. So, I need to plug in a caveat about my overall predictions about the future in this book. I could be wrong. I stand by my conclusions, of course, but certain developments could be more important than my analysis has indicated. For example, the COVID-19 pandemic and Russia's invasion of Ukraine have amplified the debate on reshoring, onshoring, friendshoring and deglobalization. In the book, I have indicated that we will see reorganization of supply chains and value chains but that globalization at large is returning to business as usual. However, ramifications could be more serious than my analysis has indicated seeing that several deglobalization dynamics are at play. In addition to the global value chain disruptions caused by COVID-19 and Russia's invasion of Ukraine, we are seeing rising trade tensions and moves towards protectionism between major trading blocks, for example, between China and the United States, as discussed. We are also seeing growing calls for localized production due to the damaging ecological footprint of international trade. Given all the dynamics at play here, 'deglobalization' could have been a separate megatrend. So, this is an additional topic worth monitoring closely in the near future.

Embracing or transcending capitalism?

Throughout the book, I have stressed that global capitalism has a tendency to be polarizing rather than equalizing. The unprecedented power amassed by transnational corporations based in the global North is a product of dynamics within capitalism. Ecological breakdown, caused by the constant pursuit of growth and capital accumulation without consideration for the natural environment, is a product of dynamics within capitalism. At the same time, I have provided countless examples of countries that have utilized capitalism to their benefit in the process of economic development— from the United States in the nineteenth century to China in recent decades. The idea that economic development is a process that benefits from capitalist dynamics is an idea that I haven't really challenged.

Is this stance towards capitalism not contradictory? Can I both embrace and shun capitalism? Let me explain how this seemingly contradictory stance makes sense. First, let's start with the critique of capitalism, its foundation (in this book), and why it's important. My critical stance towards capitalism should not be understated— after all, one of the most important arguments of the book is rooted in socialist, post-capitalist, and anti-capitalist views. This is the argument that power asymmetries in the world economy creates uneven opportunities to reap the benefits from industrialization and, at worst, makes it harder for countries in the global South to industrialize altogether.

The first part of this argument is grounded in the observation that transnational corporations mainly based on the global North— and, to some degree, the countries they are based in—are amassing power and profits at the expense of firms, workers, and sometimes entire countries in the global South. Capitalism feeds this dynamic through the type of globalization we have witnessed in the past few decades: largely unregulated globalization that has expanded the reach of these transnational corporations both in terms of markets and access to cheap inputs and wage labour. This argument has clear parallels to Marxist-inspired theories of how global capitalism works, such as dependency theory. This theory, which I mentioned earlier in the book, highlights how the world economy is characterized by resources flowing from a 'periphery' of poor states to a 'core' of wealthy states, enriching the latter at the expense of the former.

The second part of this argument is grounded in the degrowth paradigm, a paradigm drawing on, and overlapping with, the eco-socialist movement. The degrowth paradigm believes that there is a fundamental contradiction between capitalism/industrialism and ecological sustainability. Earlier in the book, I showed how, empirically, there is a good case to be made for this contradiction. Resource use and energy use have skyrocketed in today's high-income capitalist societies as capitalism is a system that fundamentally requires growth in output in order to be successful. If we accept that economic growth and industrialization go hand in hand with increased energy and resource use, the countries that have gone through this process (today's high-income countries) have limited the chance for other countries to do so (today's low-income and middle-income countries), given that the resources on our planet are finite.

From a social point of view, capitalism is clearly characterized by undesirable dynamics. But the solution isn't necessarily to ditch it. Luckily, there isn't only one type of capitalism. We see different varieties of it throughout the world, regulated in some regions more than in others. It's not like we have to choose between capitalism and socialism, as in the science-fiction action film *The Matrix*, where Neo has to choose between the red pill and the blue pill. Capitalism has become adopted and moulded in a variety of ways by different states. Some states, particularly the Nordic ones, have been able to create a variety of types of capitalism with socialist traits, in which most people enjoy a high quality of life. In these socialist versions of capitalism, there is private ownership in the economy, yes, but the state has control over the commanding heights of the economy, clamps down on unwanted monopoly and oligopoly practices in the private sector, and ensures decent labour standards and welfare services for everyone.

Turning to the history of catch-up development, we see that highly successful states have embraced capitalism but have done so on their own terms and governed capitalist markets carefully. Countries in East Asia that developed their economies at breakneck speed in the second half of the twentieth century benefited from capitalist globalization but utilized trade networks, international capital, and foreign investment to their advantage. They used a good dose of protectionism, bargained with foreign investors, and utilized state ownership in the economy to steer structural transformation of the economy in the desired direction.

Not all countries in the world will be able to emulate Nordic welfare capitalism or the East Asian developmental states. And, as I have highlighted, global capitalism has produced an unlevel playing field in the world economy. Capitalism is clearly an imperfect system that produces inequalities within and between countries, and it hopefully won't stick around forever. We are right to think about post-capitalism. But the solution isn't to abolish private capital flows or scrap lessons from capitalist development experiences. The solution is to make the playing field level, drawing on socialist and egalitarian ideas. That is why I have suggested ways to make the system of global governance truly democratic and made the case for more ecological policy space in the global South. We can create a type of capitalism that works for the many rather than the few.

Notes

Introduction

1. This analysis of the Apple value chain is recent as of 2022.
2. The IPCC is an intergovernmental body of the UN responsible for advancing knowledge on climate change.
3. https://www.blackrock.com/sg/en/investment-ideas/themes/megatrends; https://www.pwc.co.uk/issues/megatrends.html; https://www.ey.com/en_gl/megatrends (accessed 25 March 2023).
4. The fourth Industrial Revolution refers to the development and merging of technologies in the digital domain, such as (in alphabetical order) additive manufacturing, advanced robotics, artificial intelligence, big data analytics, cloud computing, the industrial internet-of-things, and machine learning.
5. The commercialization of digital technologies in the second half of the twentieth century is sometimes referred to as the 'third Industrial Revolution'. The growth of the electronics industry (e.g. the modern computer and the modern cell phone) and the growth of the internet are manifestations of this.
6. Such as Baldwin (2016); Hallward-Driemeier and Nayyar (2017).
7. Lange (2012).
8. For a more detailed presentation of the historical school of economics, see Chang (2002).
9. The reader should note that there is some overlap between the policy pillar on ecological breakdown and the chapter on ecological breakdown as this chapter is the one megatrend chapter that does actually cover policy implications.
10. https://www.nytimes.com/2022/07/27/us/politics/senate-chips-china.html (accessed 25 March 2023).
11. https://www.census.gov/newsroom/stories/poverty-awareness-month.html (accessed 25 March 2023).
12. https://data.worldbank.org (accessed 25 March 2023).

Chapter 1

1. Chernow (2004).
2. https://www.theatlantic.com/entertainment/archive/2015/09/lin-manuel-miranda-hamilton/408019 (accessed 25 March 2023).
3. Hamilton (1934 [1791]).

4. Helleiner (2021).
5. Nayyar (2013).
6. Landes (1969).
7. Landes (1969), p. 124.
8. Bairoch (1982).
9. Maddison (2007).
10. See Szirmai (2012) for a good overview of the evidence, especially since 1950.
11. Smith (1982 [1776]).
12. As detailed well by Abramowitz (1969).
13. Marx (1990 [1867]).
14. Rosenberg (1982) discusses this in length in his chapter, 'Marx as a student of technology'.
15. Babbage (2015 [1832]).
16. Andreoni and Chang (2017).
17. For their original works, see Chenery (1960); Gerschenkron (1962); Hirschman (1958); Kaldor (1967); Kuznets (1966); Lewis (1954); Myrdal (1957); Nurkse (1961); Prebisch (1950).
18. Kaldor (1967).
19. Andreoni and Chang (2016).
20. Hirschman (1958).
21. Meckstroth (2017).
22. Schumpeter (1983 [1934], 2010 [1942]). Chang (2014), Chapter 4 provides a good and brief overview of Schumpeter's central work and his legacy.
23. Leading figures of this body of work include Christopher Freeman, Bengt-Åke Lundvall, Richard Nelson, and Sidney Winter. There are shared insights between innovation studies and development economics, often bridged in the work of Nathan Rosenberg.
24. See Teece (2010) for a good overview.
25. Pisano and Shih (2012), p. 2.
26. Szreter and Mooney (1998).
27. Kohli (2020).
28. Hickel et al. (2022a).
29. Weber et al. (2021).
30. Some influential works include Amin (1974); Cardoso and Faletto (1979); Frank (1967); Prebisch (1950); Wallerstein (1974).
31. As argued by Kvangraven (2021), who provides a great synthesis of dependency theory as well as its continued relevance. For material that more broadly covers uneven economic development processes, I highly recommend Reinert and Kvangraven (2023).

32. Hickel et al. (2022a).
33. My definition of industrial policy builds on understandings of industrial policy set out in Chang (1994) and Oqubay (2015). The term 'productive capabilities' can be interpreted in the same way as 'productive capacities' in UNCTADs productive capacities index, which is: 'the productive resources, entrepreneurial capabilities and production linkages that together determine a country's ability to produce goods and services that will help it grow and develop', https://unctad.org/topic/least-developed-countries/productive-capacities-index#:~:text=%22Productive%20capacities%20are%20the%20productive,for%20the%20period%202000%2D2018 (accessed 25 March 2023).
34. Chang (2002).
35. See, e.g. Amsden (1992); Chang (1994); Wade (1990), for detailed analyses of industrial policy in South Korea and Taiwan, which are considered more generalizable in their industrial policy experiences than Hong Kong and Singapore.
36. World Bank (1993), p. 6.
37. As highlighted by, e.g. Aiginger and Rodrik (2020); Stiglitz and Lin (2013).
38. Hamilton (1934 [1791]).
39. List (2005 [1841]).
40. Mazzucato (2013).
41. Ocampo et al. (2009).
42. Nem Singh and Chen (2018).
43. Amsden (2001).
44. Amsden (1985).
45. Short (1983).
46. See, especially, Amsden (2001).
47. Helleiner (2021) provides a rich overview of the diverse intellectual contributions.
48. Helleiner (2021).
49. Chiang (2013 [1947]).
50. Solberg (1979).
51. MacDuffie (2016).
52. Okonwo (1980).
53. See Clapham (2018); Hauge and Chang (2019a).
54. Rekiso (2019); Zewde (2002).
55. Helleiner (2021).
56. Noman et al. (2011).

Chapter 2

1. https://databank.worldbank.org/source/world-development-indicators (accessed 25 March 2023).
2. Bell (1976).
3. See, e.g. Baer and Samuelson (1981); Bhagwati (1984).
4. Baldwin and Forslid (2020); Ghani and Kharas (2010); Hallward-Driemeier and Nayyar (2017); Loungani et al. (2017); Miroudot and Cadestin (2017); Nayyar et al. (2021); WTO (2019).
5. See Table 1.3 in Nayyar et al. (2021), who refer to these three groups of services as 'global innovator services'.
6. Hallward-Driemeier and Nayyar (2017); Nayyar (2013); Nayyar et al. (2021).
7. https://www.statista.com (accessed 25 March 2023).
8. WTO (2019).
9. WTO (2013).
10. Branstetter et al. (2018).
11. Nayyar et al. (2021).
12. Nayyar et al. (2018).
13. McMillan et al. (2017).
14. Botsworth and Collins (2008).
15. WTO (2019).
16. McMillan et al. (2017).
17. UNECA (2015).
18. Chang et al. (2013).
19. Andreoni and Chang (2016).
20. Park and Chan (1989).
21. Pilat and Wolfl (2005).
22. Kuan (2017).
23. Bonvillian and Singer (2018).
24. Nayyar et al. (2021).
25. Hirschman (1958).
26. Kaldor (1967).
27. Baumol and Bowen (1965).
28. See Chapter 2 for a more detailed analysis of the history of industrialization.
29. Botswana has amassed its wealth from precious stones (diamonds), while Oman has done so through oil.
30. World Bank (2008).
31. Marconi et al. (2016).
32. See, e.g. Andreoni and and Chang (2017); Nayyar (2013); Szirmai (2012); Szirmai and Verspagen (2015).

33. Neither Botswana nor Oman are mentioned, as their current level of GDP per capita arguably does not qualify for having achieved 'high and sustainable standards of living'.

34. https://www.nytimes.com/2022/07/27/us/politics/senate-chips-china.html (accessed 25 March 2023).

35. https://www.chathamhouse.org/events/all/members-event/future-liberal-democracies-conversation-william-hague-and-hillary-clinton (accessed 25 March 2023).

36. Gervais and Jensen (2019).

37. Nayyar et al. (2021).

38. https://databank.worldbank.org/source/world-development-indicators (accessed 25 March 2023).

39. https://www.statista.com (accessed 25 March 2023).

40. Chang et al. (2016b).

41. WTO (2019).

42. https://databank.worldbank.org/source/world-development-indicators (accessed 25 March 2023).

43. Miroudot and Cadestin (2017).

44. See Hauge and O'Sullivan (2019) for a more comprehensive discussion.

45. Hauge and O'Sullivan (2019).

46. Bamber et al. (2017).

47. Hauge and O'Sullivan (2019).

48. Whitefoot et al. (2015).

49. Hauge (2021).

50. Hauge and O'Sullivan (2019).

51. Berger (2015); Pisano and Shih (2012).

52. Manufacturing Metrics Expert Group (2016).

53. Chang (2014), chapter 7.

54. Chang (2014), chapter 7.

55. Rowthorn and Ramaswamy (1999).

56. Tregenna (2009).

57. Cramer et al. (2022).

58. Haraguchi et al. (2017).

Chapter 3

1. Allen (2009); Manyika et al. (2017b).

2. Manyika et al. (2017b).

3. Autor et al. (2015).

4. Acemoglu and Restrepo (2019).
5. See, e.g. Brynjolfsson and McAfee (2014); Ford (2015); Frey and Osborne (2017); Schwab (2016); Susskind and Susskind (2015).
6. Chang et al. (2016a); Frey and Rabhari (2016); World Bank (2016).
7. Baldwin and Forslid (2020); Hallward-Driemeier and Nayyar (2017); Manyika et al. (2017a); Schlogl and Sumner (2020).
8. Andreoni and Anzolin (2019).
9. Bessen (2016, 2019).
10. Manyika et al (2017b).
11. Manyika et al (2017b).
12. Autor et al. (2015).
13. Bessen (2016).
14. Acemoglu and Restrepo (2019); Brynjolfsson and McAfee (2014); Chiacchio et al. (2018); Piva and Vivarelli (2017).
15. Autor et al. (2015).
16. Miller and Atkinson (2013).
17. Miller and Atkinson (2013).
18. Acemoglu and Restrepo (2020); Dauth et al. (2017); Mann and Püttman (2018).
19. Dauth et al. (2017).
20. Mann and Püttman (2018).
21. UNIDO (2020).
22. Asian Development Bank (2018).
23. Dutz et al. (2018).
24. Asian Development Bank (2018); UNCTAD (2017); UNIDO (2020); World Bank (2016)
25. UNCTAD (2017), p. 39.
26. Parschau and Hauge (2020).
27. Willcocks (2020).
28. McKinsey (2018).
29. UNIDO (2020).
30. Frey and Osborne (2017).
31. https://www.pastemagazine.com/movies/robots/the-100-greatest-movie-robots-of-all-time (accessed 25 March 2023).
32. Arntz et al. (2016).
33. Chang et al. (2016a); Frey and Osborne (2017); Manyika et al (2017a).
34. Nayak and Padhye (2017); Parschau and Hauge (2020).
35. Manyika et al. (2017a).
36. Manyika et al. (2017b).
37. World Economic Forum (2020).
38. PwC (2017).
39. World Bank (2016).

40. Kinkel and Maloca (2009), p. 155.
41. Gray et al. (2013); Hallward-Driemeier and Nayyar (2017).
42. https://qz.com/1746152/adidas-is-shutting-down-its-speedfactories-in-germany-and-the-us (accessed 25 March 2023).
43. Dachs et al. (2019).
44. Dachs and Seric (2019).
45. Bailey and De Propris (2014); Dachs and Seric (2019); Dachs et al. (2019); Ellram et al. (2013); Tate (2014).
46. https://www.ft.com/content/8127dbfd-a464-4ee5-9581-ff1edb22e20c?emailId=6281cc4cb2ad610023fdb2ce&segmentId=22011ee7-896a-8c4c-22a0-7603348b7f22 (accessed 25 March 2023).
47. Make UK (2022).
48. https://www.wto.org/english/news_e/pres21_e/pr889_e.htm (accessed 25 March 2023).
49. https://www.wto.org/english/news_e/pres22_e/pr909_e.htm (accessed 25 March 2023).

Chapter 4

1. Hauge (2020).
2. Baldwin (2016); OECD (2013).
3. Many related terms are used to refer to global production systems, but I will stick to the most commonly used one, which is global value chains. I will make distinctions between terms when necessary.
4. Ricardo's example was a simplified version of the world, which not only featured cloth and wine as the only traded products but also Britain and Portugal as the only countries.
5. See, e.g. Baldwin (2011, 2016); Cattaneo et al. (2013); Milberg et al (2014); Taglioni and Winkler (2016); World Bank (2020).
6. See, e.g. Baldwin (2011, 2016); Hauge (2020); Kaplinsky and Morris (2016); Milberg and Winkler (2013); Milberg et al. (2014); Morris and Staritz (2019); Taglioni and Winkler (2016); World Bank (2020).
7. Farole and Winkler (2014); Hauge (2020); OECD (2002, 2013); Taglioni and Winkler (2016); World Bank (2020).
8. Referring to Hong Kong, Singapore, South Korea, and Taiwan, which have all achieved rapid economic growth and industrialization since 1960.
9. Hauge (2020).
10. Pisano and Shih (2012); https://www.nytimes.com/2022/07/27/us/politics/senate-chips-china.html (accessed 25 March 2023).
11. Baldwin (2011, 2016); Cattaneo et al. (2013); OECD (2013).
12. Baldwin (2011).

13. UNCTAD (2019).
14. Gereffi and Lee (2012).
15. As argued by, e.g. Bair et al. (2021); Selwyn and Leyden (2022).
16. Farole and Winkler (2014); Görg and Greenway (2004). https://elibrary.worldbank.org/doi/10.1093/wbro/lkh019; Paus and Gallagher (2008).
17. Milberg and Winkler (2013).
18. Paus and Gallagher (2008).
19. Palacios (2001); Wilson (1992).
20. Paus and Gallagher (2008).
21. Paus and Gallagher (2008).
22. Gallagher and Zarsky (2007).
23. Gallagher and Zarsky (2007).
24. Roberts and Lamp (2021).
25. Gallagher and Zarsky (2007), p. 9.
26. Hauge and Chang (2019b).
27. World Economic Forum (2020).
28. Anner (2020); Durand and Milberg (2020); Milberg and Winkler (2013); Nolan et al. (2008); Pagano (2014); Selwyn (2019); Selwyn and Leyden (2022); Starrs (2014); Suwandi (2019); Wade (2019).
29. Hauge (2021).
30. Nolan et al. (2008); Hauge (2020).
31. Starrs (2014).
32. Slaughter (2010).
33. https://www.theguardian.com/business/2010/jan/12/walmart-companies-to-shape-the-decade (accessed 25 March 2023).
34. Wade (2019).
35. Milberg (2008).
36. Milberg and Winkler (2013).
37. See Durand and Milberg (2020); Pagano (2014); Wade (2019) for good discussions on this.
38. Durand and Milberg (2020).
39. Durand and Milberg (2020), p. 414.
40. International Labour Organization (2020).
41. International Labour Organization (2020).
42. Selwyn (2017), p. 54
43. Anner (2020); Chan (2013); Mezzadri (2016); Selwyn (2019); Selwyn and Leyden (2022).
44. Selwyn (2019).
45. Deyo (1989).
46. Hardy and Hauge (2019).

47. The first part of the quote is from this sub-tab: https://www.wto.org/english/thewto_e/whatis_e/who_we_are_e.htm. The second part of the quote is from this sub-tab: https://www.wto.org/english/thewto_e/whatis_e/what_stand_for_e.htm (accessed 25 March 2023).
48. Hamilton (1934 [1791]).
49. Chang (2002).
50. As highlighted by, e.g. Chang (2002, 2007); Reinert (2007).
51. Chang et al. (2016b); Mayer (2009); Shadlen (2005); Wade (2003, 2019).
52. Gallagher (2007); Gallagher and Kozul-Wright (2022).
53. Chang et al. (2016b).
54. These rules broadly fall under the General Agreement on Tariffs and Trade (GATT)—an agreement that was the precursor to the establishment of the WTO and which is still under effect within the WTO framework—the General Agreement on Trade in Services (GATS) and the Agreement on Trade Related Investment Measures (TRIMS).
55. Gallagher and Kozul-Wright (2022).
56. Wade (2003, 2019).
57. https://the.ink/p/doses-are-charity-knowledge-is-justice?triedSigningIn=true (accessed 25 March 2023).
58. Gallagher (2008); Gallagher and Kozul-Wright (2022); Shadlen (2005).
59. UNIDO (2022) provides a detailed explanation of how global production was halted by the pandemic in a number of different ways.
60. https://www.ft.com/content/3f4a1579-2733-40e9-b052-cb0629296765 (accessed 25 March 2023).
61. Authors calculations based on data from UNCTAD Data Center.
62. See, e.g. Antràs (2020); Baldwin and Di Mauro (2020); Gereffi (2020); UNCTAD (2020); UNIDO (2022).
63. UNCTAD (2020).
64. https://unctad.org/news/how-covid-19-changing-global-value-chains (accessed 25 March 2023).
65. https://blogs.worldbank.org/developmenttalk/commodity-prices-surge-due-war-ukraine (accessed 25 March 2023).
66. https://www.bloomberg.com/opinion/articles/2021-12-05/omicron-sounds-death-knell-for-globalization-2-0; https://www.newstatesman.com/long-reads/2020/04/coronavirus-crisis-has-sounded-death-knell-liberal-globalisation (accessed 25 March 2023).
67. Foroohar (2022).
68. Data on trade: https://www.wto.org/english/news_e/pres22_e/pr902_e.htm. Data on investment: https://unctad.org/news/global-foreign-investment-recovered-pre-pandemic-levels-2021-uncertainty-looms (accessed 25 March 2023). A caveat to this recovery is that supply-chain bottlenecks still exist and

that new investment projects (greenfield investment) in developing countries are at low levels.

69. Cheng and Li (2022).
70. Selwyn (2019); Suwandi (2019).
71. Weber et al. (2021); World Bank (2020).
72. Hickel (2017).

Chapter 5

1. The IPCC is an intergovernmental body of the UN responsible for advancing knowledge on climate change.
2. IPCC (2022).
3. https://www.worldbank.org/en/news/press-release/2022/10/28/pakistan-flood-damages-and-economic-losses-over-usd-30-billion-and-reconstruction-needs-over-usd-16-billion-new-assessme (accessed 25 March 2023).
4. https://ourworldindata.org/deforestation (accessed 25 March 2023).
5. https://www.theguardian.com/environment/2022/apr/27/united-nations-40-per-cent-planet-land-degraded (accessed 25 March 2023).
6. https://unctad.org/news/90-fish-stocks-are-used-fisheries-subsidies-must-stop (accessed 25 March 2023).
7. WWF (2018).
8. https://fee.org/articles/the-great-horse-manure-crisis-of-1894 (accessed 25 March 2023).
9. For comprehensive discussion on green growth, see, e.g. Anzolin and Lebdioui (2021); Dale et al. (2016); Hickel and Kallis (2020); Jacobs (2013); Pollin (2015).
10. Hallegatte et al. (2012); World Bank (2012).
11. Pollin (2015).
12. Garrett-Peltier (2017), as reported in Anzolin and Lebdioui (2021).
13. See Ajl (2021); Chomsky and Pollin (2020); Pettifor (2019); Rifkin (2019), for Green New Deal proposals.
14. https://www.vox.com/energy-and-environment/2019/2/7/18211709/green-new-deal-resolution-alexandria-ocasio-cortez-markey (accessed 25 March 2023).
15. Chomsky and Pollin (2020).
16. Some important works on green industrial policy include Altenburg and Assman (2017); Anzolin and Lebdiou (2021); Hallegatte et al. (2013); Rodrik (2014).
17. Altenburg and Assmann (2017) provide numerous case studies in their edited volume.

18. Anzolin and Lebdiou (2021); Batinge et al. (2017); Jacobs (2013); Lee (2019).
19. Pilling (2019) has a great chapter on how GDP became something bigger and nastier than Kuznets intended, drawing parallels to Frankenstein's monster (the chapter is entitled 'Kuznets' monster').
20. Nussbaum and Sen (1993).
21. Like the Human Development Index, the OECD Better Life Index, the Happiness Index, and the Happy Planet Index.
22. IPCC (2022), p. 105 in chapter 5.
23. Daly (1973); Georgescu-Roegen (1971); Meadows et al. (1972).
24. Weiss and Cattaneo (2017).
25. Kallis et al. (2020).
26. Hickel (2021).
27. Schmeltzer et al. (2022).
28. Steinmann et al. (2017).
29. For data on material footprint, resource use, and ecological overshoot of nations, see, e.g. Fanning et al. (2022); Hickel (2020); Hickel and Kallis (2020); Hickel et al. (2022b).
30. Bringezu (2015).
31. Gregoir and Acker (2022).
32. Hickel (2020).
33. WWF (2021).
34. Hickel (2020).
35. https://www.c2es.org/content/renewable-energy/#:~:text=Globally%2C%20renewables%20made%20up%2029,was%20added%20globally%20during%202020 (accessed 25 March 2023).
36. Hickel et al. (2022b).
37. Hauge (2020).
38. Horner and Nadvi (2018).
39. Hickel et al. (2022b).
40. See Wiedmann and Lenzen (2018) for a good analysis of the ecological impact of international trade.
41. https://www.theguardian.com/environment/2021/sep/28/blah-greta-thunberg-leaders-climate-crisis-co2-emissions (accessed 25 March 2023).
42. Newman et al. (2020). Keep in mind that these numbers represent averages and therefore do not capture variation from the mean. For example, in the United States, 12% of people said climate change is not serious at all. This is a significant deviation from the global average of 3%.
43. Löwy et al. (2022).
44. Schmeltzer et al. (2022).
45. Lenaerts et al. (2022), p.1.
46. https://fullfact.org/economy/do-15-people-take-70-flights (accessed 25 March 2023).

47. https://weareyard.com/insights/worst-celebrity-private-jet-co2-emission-offenders (accessed 25 March 2023).

48. https://www.dw.com/en/superyachts-symbolize-climate-breakdown/a-61245302#:~:text=The%20top%2020%20billionaires%20analyzed,are%20created%20by%20their%20superyachts (accessed 25 March 2023).

49. https://england.shelter.org.uk/support_us/campaigns/social_housing_deficit (accessed 25 March 2023).

Chapter 6

1. With the exception of the chapter on ecological breakdown, in which I discussed policy proposals as well.

2. Baldwin (2011), p. 3.

3. In Hauge (2020) you can read in greater detail about these policies in the cases of South Korea and Taiwan.

4. See Cramer et al. (2022) for a great discussion on the role of high-value agriculture in industrialization.

5. Georgieff and Milanez (2021).

6. Manyika et al. (2017b).

7. Bechichi et al. (2019).

8. UNIDO (2020).

9. UNCTAD (2017).

10. Gallagher and Kozul-Wright (2022).

11. A proposition by Hickel (2017).

12. https://www.theguardian.com/lifeandstyle/2022/may/13/global-minimum-wage-ask-an-expert (accessed 25 March 2023).

13. These are goods that use imported inputs, which is a key measure of participation in global value chains.

14. Horner and Alford (2019).

15. Pollin (2020).

16. Hickel et al. (2022b).

17. Paraphrasing Hickel (2020).

18. https://blogs.worldbank.org/developmenttalk/commodity-prices-surge-due-war-ukraine (accessed 25 March 2023).

Conclusion

1. See Altenburg et al. (2021), who identify global economic power shifts as a megatrend impacting industrialization pathways.

2. UNIDO (2022).

3. Andreoni and Roberts (2022).

4. Zuboff (2019).

References

Abramowitz, M. (1969). *Thinking about Growth: And Other Essays on Economic Growth and Welfare*. Cambridge: Cambridge University Press.

Acemoglu, D. and Restrepo, P. (2019). 'The Wrong Kind of AI? Artificial Intelligence and the Future of Labour Demand', *Cambridge Journal of Regions, Economy and Society*, 13/1: 25–35.

Acemoglu, D. and Restrepo, P. (2020). 'Robots and Jobs: Evidence from US Labor Markets', *Journal of Political Economy*, 128/6: 2188–2244.

Aiginger, K. and Rodrik, D. (2020). 'Rebirth of Industrial Policy and an Agenda for the Twenty-First Century', *Journal of Industry, Competition and Trade*, 20/2: 189–207.

Ajl, M. (2021). *A People's Green New Deal*. London: Pluto Press.

Allen, R.C. (2009). 'Engels' Pause: Technical Change, Capital Accumulation, and Inequality in the British Industrial Revolution', *Explorations in Economic History*, 46/4: 418–435.

Altenburg, T. and Assmann, C. (eds) (2017). *Green Industrial Policy: Concept, Policies, Country Experiences*. Geneva, Bonn: UN Environment, German Development Institute.

Altenburg, T., Feng, K., and Shen, Q. (2017). 'Electric Mobility and the Quest for Automobile Industry Upgrading in China', in T. Altenburg and C. Assmann (eds), *Green Industrial Policy: Concept, Policies, Country Experiences*. Geneva, Bonn: UN Environment, German Development Institute, pp. 185–198.

Altenburg, T., Brandi, C., Pegels, A., Stamm, A., Vrolijk, K., and Zintl, T. (2021). 'COVID-19: Turning Point in the Process of Industrialization?', UN Industrial Development Organization, Working Paper No. 8/2021.

Amin, S. (1974). *Accumulation on a World Scale: A Critique of the Theory of Underdevelopment*. New York: Monthly Review Press.

Amsden, A.H. (1985). 'The State and Taiwan's Economic Development', in P. Evans, D. Ruschmeyer, and T. Skocpol (eds), *Brining the State Back In*. Cambridge: Cambridge University Press, pp. 78–106.

Amsden, A.H. (1992). *Asia's Next Giant: South Korea and Late Industrialization*. Oxford and New York: Oxford University Press.

Amsden, A.H. (2001). *The Rise of "The Rest": Challenges to the West from Late-Industrializing Economies*. Oxford and New York: Oxford University Press.

Andreoni, A. and Anzolin, G. (2019). 'A revolution in the Making? Challenges and opportunities of digital production technologies for developing countries', UN Industrial Development Organization, Inclusive and Sustainable Industrial Development Working Paper Series, WP 7.

Andreoni, A. and Chang, H.-J. (2016). 'Industrial Policy and the Future of Manufacturing', *Economia e Politica Industriale*, 43/4: 491–502.

Andreoni, A. and Chang, H.-J. (2017). 'Bringing Production and Employment Back into Development: Alice Amsden's Legacy for a New Developmentalist Agenda', *Cambridge Journal of Regions, Economy and Society*, 10/1: 173–187.

Andreoni, A. and Roberts, A. (2022). 'Governing Digital Platform Power for Industrial Development: Towards an Entrepreneurial-Regulatory State', *Cambridge Journal of Economics* (online first), https://academic.oup.com/cje/article/46/6/1431/6832143.

Anner, M. (2020). 'Squeezing Workers' Rights in Global Supply Chains: Purchasing Practices in the Bangladesh Garment Export Sector in Comparative Perspective', *Review of International Political Economy*, 27/2: 320–347.

Antràs, P. (2020). 'De-globalisation? Global Value Chains in the Post-COVID-19 Age', NBER Working Paper No. 28115.

Anzolin, G. and Lebdioui, A. (2021). 'Three Dimensions of Green Industrial Policy in the Context of Climate Change and Sustainable Development', *European Journal of Development Research*, 33/2: 371–405.

Arntz, M., Gregory, T. and Zierahn, U. (2016). 'The Risk of Automation for Jobs in OECD Countries: A Comparative Analysis', Organisation for Economic Co-operation and Development (OECD) Social, Employment and Migration Working Papers No. 189. Paris: OECD.

Asian Development Bank (2018). *Asian Development Outlook 2018: How Technology Affects Jobs*. Manila: Asian Development Bank.

Autor, D.H., Doen, D. and Hanson, G.H. (2015). 'Untangling Trade and Technology: Evidence from Local Labour Markets', *Economic Journal*, 125/584: 621–646.

Babbage, C. (2015[1832]). *On the Economy of Machinery and Manufactures*. New York: Palala Press.

Baer, W. and Samuelson, L (1981). 'Toward a Service-Oriented Growth Strategy', *World Development*, 9/6: 499–514.

Bairoch, P. (1982). 'International Industrialization Levels from 1750 to 1980', *Journal of European Economic History*, 11/2: 269.

Bailey, D. and De Propris, L. (2014). 'Manufacturing Reshoring and Its Limits: The UK Automotive Case', *Cambridge Journal of Regions, Economy, and Society*. 7/3: 379–395.

Bair, J., Mahutga, M., Werner, M., and Campling, L. (2021). 'Capitalist Crisis in the "Age of Global Value Chains"', *Environment and Planning A: Economy and Space*, 53/6: 1253–1272.

Baldwin, R. (2011). 'Trade and Industrialisation after Globalisation's 2nd Unbundling: How Building and Joining a Supply Chain Are Different and Why It Matters', National Bureau of Economic Research (NBER) Working Paper No. 17716.

Baldwin, R. (2016). *The Great Convergence: Information Technology and the New Globalization*. Cambridge (MA): Harvard University Press.

Baldwin, R. and Di Mauro, B.W. (2020). *Economics in the Time of COVID-19: A New eBook*. VOX CEPR Policy Portal.

Baldwin, R. and Forslid, R. (2020). 'Globotics and Development: When Manufacturing Is Jobless and Services are Tradable', NBER Working Paper No. 26731.

Bamber, P. Cattaneo, O., Fernandez-Stark, K., Gereffi, G., Van der Marel, E. and Sheperd, B. (2017). "Diversification through servification." World Bank: Washington D.C

Batinge, B., Musango, J.K., and Brent, A.C. (2017). 'Leapfrogging to Renewable Energy: The Opportunity for Unmet Electricity Markets', *South African Journal of Industrial Engineering*, 28/4: 32–49.

Baumol, W.J. and Bowen, W.G. (1965). 'On the Performing Arts: The Anatomy of Their Economic Problems', *American Economic Review*, 55/1: 495–502.

Bechichi, N., Jamet, S., Kenedi, G., Grundke, R., and Squicciarini, M. (2019). 'Occupational Mobility, Skills and Training Needs ', OECD Science, Technology and Industrial Policy Papers. Paris: OECD.

Bell, D. (1976). *The Coming of Post-Industrial Society*. New York: Basic Books.

Berger, S. (2015). *Making in America: From Innovation to Market*. Cambridge (MA): MIT Press.

Bessen, J.E. (2016). 'How Computer Automation Affects Occupations: Technology, Jobs, and Skills', Law and Economics Research Paper, Boston University School of Law.

Bessen, J. (2019). 'Automation and Jobs: When Technology Boosts Employment', *Economic Policy*, 34/100: 589–626.

Bhagwati, J.N. (1984). 'Splintering and Disembodiment of Services and Developing Nations', *World Economy*, 7/2: 133–144.

Botsworth, B. and Collins, S.M. (2008). 'Accounting for Growth: Comparing China and India', *Journal of Economic Perspectives*, 22/1: 45–66.

Bonvillian, W.B. and Singer, P.L. (2018). *Advanced Manufacturing: The New American Innovation Policies*. Cambridge (MA): MIT Press.

Branstetter, L., Glennon, B., and Jensen, J.B. (2018). 'Knowledge Transfer Abroad: The Role of US Inventors within Global R&D Networks', NBER Working Paper No. 24453.

Bringezu, S. (2015). 'Possible Target Corridor for Sustainable Use of Global Material Resources', *Resources*, 4/1: 25–54.

Brynjolfsson, E. and McAfee, A. (2014). *The Second Machine Age: Work, Progress, and Prosperity in a Time of Brilliant Technologies*. New York: W.W. Norton & Company.

Cardoso, F.H. and Faletto, E. (1979). *Dependency and Development in Latin America*. Los Angeles (CA): University of California Press.

Cattaneo, O., Gereffi, G., Miroudot, S., and Taglioni, D. (2013). 'Joining, Upgrading and Being Competitive in Global Value Chains: A Strategic Framework', World Bank Policy Research Working Paper No. 6406.

Chan, J. (2013). 'A Suicide Survivor: The Life of a Chinese Worker', *New Technology, Work and Employment*, 28/2: 84–99.

Chang, H.-J. (1994). *The Political Economy of Industrial Policy*. Basingstoke: Macmillan Press.

Chang, H.-J. (2002). *Kicking Away the Ladder: Development Strategy in Historical Perspective*. London: Anthem Press.

Chang, H.-J. (2007). *Bad Samaritans: The Myth of Free Trade and the Secret History of Capitalism*. London: Bloomsbury Publishing.

Chang, H.-J. (2014). *Economics: The User's Guide*. London, New York: Pelican Books.

Chang, H.-J., Andreoni, A., and Kuan, M.L. (2013). 'International Industrial Policy Experiences and Lessons for the UK', UK Government Office for Science.

Chang, J.H., Rynhart, G., and Huynh, P. (2016a). 'ASEAN in Transformation: Textiles, Clothing and Footwear: Refashioning the Future', Working Paper No. 14. Geneva: International Labour Organization.

Chang, H.-J., Hauge, J., and Irfan, M. (2016b). *Transformative Industrial Policy for Africa*. Addis Ababa: United Nations Economic Commission for Africa.

Chenery, H. (1960). 'Patterns of Industrial Growth', *American Economic Review*, 50: 624–654.

Cheng, T.-F. and Li, L. (2022). 'The Resilience Myth: Fatal Flaws in the Push to Secure Chip Supply Chains', *Nikkei Asia*, 27 July.

Chernow, R. (2004). *Alexander Hamilton*. London, New York: Penguin Random House.

Chiacchio, F., Petropoulos, G., and Pichler, D. (2018). 'The Impact of Industrial Robots on EU Employment and Wages: A Local Labour Market Approach', Bruegel Working Paper No. 02/2018.

Chiang, K.-S. (2013[1947]). *China's Destiny and Chinese Economic Theory*. Leiden: Global Oriental.

Chomsky, N. and Pollin, R. (2020). *Climate Crisis and the Global Green New Deal*. London, New York: Verso Books.

Clapham, C. (2018). 'The Ethiopian Developmental State', *Third World Quarterly*, 39/6: 1151–1165.

Cramer, C., Di John, J., and Sender, J. (2022). 'Classification and Roundabout Production in High-Value Agriculture: A Fresh Approach to Industrialization', *Development and Change*, 53/3: 495–524.

Dachs, Bernhard and Seric, Adnan. (2019) "Industry 4.0 and the changing topography of global value chains." Inclusive and Sustainable Industrial Development Working Paper Series 10/2019. Vienna: UNIDO

Dachs, B., Kinkel, S., and Jäger, A. (2019). 'Bringing It All Back Home? Backshoring of Manufacturing Activities and the Adoption of Industry 4.0 Technologies', *Journal of World Business*, 54/6: 101017.

Dale, G., Mathai, M.V., and de Oliveira, J.A.P. (eds) (2016). *Green Growth: Ideology, Political Economy and the Alternatives*. London: Zed Books.

Daly, H. (1973). *Toward a Steady-State Economy*. New York: W.H. Freeman and Company.

Dauth, W., Findeisen, S., Südekum, J., and Woessner, N. (2017). 'German Robots: The Impact of Industrial Robots on Workers', CEPR Discussion Papers No. 12306.

Deyo, F.C. (1989). *Beneath the Miracle: Labor Subordination in the New Asian Industrialism*. Berkeley (CA): University of California Press.

Durand, C. and Milberg, W. (2020). 'Intellectual Monopoly in Global Value Chains'. *Review of International Political Economy*, 27/2: 404–429.

Dutz, M.A., Almeida, R.K. and Packard, T.G. (2018). *The Jobs of Tomorrow: Technology, Productivity, and Prosperity in Latin America and the Caribbean*. Washington DC: World Bank Publications.

Ellram, L.M., Tate, W.L., and Petersen, K.J. (2013), 'Offshoring and Reshoring: An Update on the Manufacturing Location Decision', *Journal of Supply Chain Management*. 49/2: 14–22.

Fanning, A.L., O'Neill, D.W., Hickel, J., and Roux, N. (2022). 'The Social Shortfall and Ecological Overshoot of Nations', *Nature Sustainability*, 5/1: 26–36.

Farole, T. and Winkler, D. (eds) (2014). *Making Foreign Direct Investment Work for Sub-Saharan Africa: Local Spillovers and Competitiveness in Global Value Chains*. Washington, DC: World Bank.

Ford, M. (2015). *The Rise of the Robots: Technology and the Threat of Mass Unemployment*. London: Oneworld Publications.

Foroohar, R. (2022). *Homecoming: The Path to Prosperity in a Post-Global World*. London, New York: Penguin Random House.

Frank, A.G. (1967). *Capitalism and Underdevelopment in Latin America: Historical Studies of Chile and Brazil*. New York: Monthly Review Press.

Frey, C.B. and Osborne, M.A. (2017). 'The Future of Employment: How Susceptible Are Jobs to Computerisation?', *Technological Forecasting and Social Change*, 114: 254–280.

Frey, C.B. and Rahbari, E. (2016). 'Do Labor-Saving Technologies Spell the Death of Jobs in the Developing World?', prepared for the 2016 Brookings Blum Roundtable.

Gallagher, K.P. (2007). 'Understanding Developing Country Resistance to the Doha Round', *Review of International Political Economy*, 15/1: 62–85.

Gallagher, K.P. (2008). 'Trading Away the Ladder? Trade Politics and Economic Development in the Americas', *New Political Economy*, 13/1: 37–59.

Gallagher, K.P. and Kozul-Wright, R. (2022). *The Case for a New Bretton Woods*. Cambridge (MA): Polity Press.

Gallagher, K.P. and Zarsky, L. (2007). *The Enclave Economy: Foreign Investment and Sustainable Development in Mexico's Silicon Valley*. Cambridge (MA): MIT Press.

Garrett-Peltier, H. (2017). 'Green versus Brown: Comparing the Employment Impacts of Energy Efficiency, Renewable Energy, and Fossil Fuels Using an Input–Output Model', *Economic Modelling*, 61: 439–447.

Georgescu-Roegen, N. (1971). *The Entropy Law and the Economic Process*. Cambridge (MA): Harvard University Press.

Georgieff, A. and Milanez, A. (2021). 'What Happened to Jobs at High Risk of Automation?', OECD Social, Employment and Migration Working Papers No. 255. Paris: OECD.

Gereffi, G. (2020). 'What Does the COVID-19 Pandemic Teach Us about Global Value Chains? The Case of Medical Supplies', *Journal of International Business Policy*, 3/3: 287–301.

Gereffi, G. and Lee, J. (2012). 'Why the World Suddenly Cares about Global Supply Chains', *Journal of Supply Chain Management*, 48/3: 24–32.

Gerschenkron, A. (1962). *Economic Backwardness in Historical Perspective*. Cambridge (MA): Harvard University Press.

Gervais, A. and Jensen, J.B. (2019). 'The Tradability of Services: Geographic Concentration and Trade Costs', *Journal of International Economics*, 118: 331–350.

Ghani, E. and Kharas, H. (2010). 'The Service Revolution ', Economic Premise No. 14, Washington, DC: World Bank.

Görg and Greenway (2004). https://elibrary.worldbank.org/doi/10.1093/wbro/lkh019.

Gray, J.V., Skowronski, K., Esenduran, G., and Rungtusanatham, M. (2013). 'The Reshoring Phenomenon: What Supply Chain Academics Ought to Know and Should Do', *Journal of Supply Chain Management*, 49/2: 27–33.

Gregoir, L. and van Acker, K. (2022). *Metals for Clean Energy: Pathways to Solving Europe's Raw Materials Challenge*. Leuven: KU Leuven and Eurometaux.

Hallegatte, S., Heal, G., Fay, M., and Treguer, D. (2012). 'From Growth to Green Growth: A Framework', NBER Working Paper No. 17841.

Hallegatte, S., Fay, M., and Vogt-Schilb, A. (2013). 'Green Industrial Policies: When and How', Policy Research Working Paper No. 6677. Washington, DC: World Bank.

Hallward-Driemeier, M. and Nayyar, G. (2017). *Trouble in the Making? The Future of Manufacturing-Led Development*. Washington, DC: World Bank.

Hamilton, A. (1934 [1791]). 'Report on the Subject of Manufactures: Communication to the House of Representatives Dec. 5, 1791 '. New York: Cosimo.

Haraguchi, N., Cheng, C.F.C., and Smeets, E. (2017). 'The Importance of Manufacturing in Economic Development: Has This Changed? *World Development*, 93: 293–315.

Hardy, V. and Hauge, J. (2019). 'Labour Challenges in Ethiopia's Textile and Leather Industries: No Voice, No Loyalty, No Exit?', *African Affairs*, 118/473: 712–736.

Hauge, J. (2020). 'Industrial Policy in the Era of Global Value Chains: Towards a Developmentalist Framework Drawing on the Industrialisation Experiences of South Korea and Taiwan', *World Economy*, 43/8: 2070–2092.

Hauge, J. (2021). 'Manufacturing-Led Development in the Digital Age: How Power Trumps Technology', *Third World Quarterly*(Online first). DOI: https://doi.org/10.1080/01436597.2021.2009739.

Hauge, J. and Chang, H.-J. (2019a). 'The Concept of a "Developmental State" in Ethiopia', in F. Cheru, C. Cramer and A. Oqubay (eds), *The Oxford Handbook of the Ethiopian Economy*. Oxford and New York: Oxford University Press, pp. 824–841.

Hauge, J. and Chang, H.-J. (2019b). 'The Role of Manufacturing versus Services in Economic Development', in P. Bianchi, C.R. Duran, and S. Labory (eds), *Transforming Industrial Policy for the Digital Age*. Cheltenham: Edward Elgar, pp. 12–36.

Hauge, J. and O'Sullivan, E. (2019). *Inside the Black Box of Manufacturing: Conceptualising and Counting Manufacturing in the Economy*. Cambridge: University of Cambridge Engineering Department.

Helleiner, E. (2021). *The Neomercantilists: A Global Intellectual History*. Ithaca (NY): Cornell University Press.

Hickel, J. (2017). *The Divide: A Brief Guide to Global Inequality and its Solutions*. London, New York: Penguin Random House.

Hickel, J. (2020). *Less Is More: How Degrowth Will Save the World*. London, New York: Penguin Random House.

Hickel, J. (2021). 'What Does Degrowth Mean? A Few Points of Clarification', *Globalizations*, 18/7: 1105–1111.

Hickel, J. and Kallis, G. (2020). 'Is Green Growth Possible?', *New Political Economy*, 25/4: 469–486.

Hickel, J. and Hallegatte, S. (2022). 'Can We Live within Environmental Limits and Still Reduce Poverty? Degrowth or Decoupling?', *Development Policy Review*, 40/1: e12584.

Hickel, J., Dorninger, C., Wieland, H., and Suwandi, I. (2022a). 'Imperialist Appropriation in the World Economy: Drain from the Global South through Unequal Exchange, 1990–2015', *Global Environmental Change*, 73: 102467.

Hickel, J., O'Neill, D.W., Fanning, A.L., and Zoomkawala, H. (2022b). 'National Responsibility for Ecological Breakdown: A Fair-Shares Assessment of Resource Use, 1970–2017', *Lancet Planetary Health*, 6/4: E342–E349.

Hirschman, A.O. (1958). *The Strategy of Economic Development*. New Haven (CT): Yale University Press.

Horner, R. and Alford, M. (2019). 'The Roles of the State in Global Value Chains', in S. Ponte, G. Gereffi, and G. Raj-Reichert (eds), *Handbook on Global Value Chains*. Cheltenham: Edward Elgar, pp. 555–569.

Horner, R. and Nadvi, K. (2018). 'Global Value Chains and the Rise of the Global South: Unpacking Twenty-First Century Polycentric Trade', *Global Networks*, 18/2: 207–237.

International Labour Organization (2020). World Employment and Social Outlook: Trends 2020. Geneva: International Labour Organization.

IPCC (Intergovernmental Panel on Climate Change) (2022). *Climate Change 2022: Mitigation of Climate Change: Working Group III Contribution to the Sixth Assessment Report of the Intergovernmental Panel on Climate Change*. Geneva: United Nations Environment Programme and World Meteorological Organization.

Jacobs, M. (2013). 'Green Growth', in R. Falkner (ed.), *The Handbook of Global Climate and Environment Policy*. Hoboken (NJ): Wiley Blackwell.

Kaldor, N. (1967). *Strategic Factors in Economic Development*. Ithaca (NY): New York State School of Industrial and Labour Relations, Cornell University.

Kallis, G., Paulson, S., D'Alisa, G., and Demaria, F. (2020). *The Case for Degrowth*. Cambridge (MA): Polity Press.

Kaplinsky, R. and Morris, M. (2016). 'Thinning and Thickening: Productive Sector Policies in the Era of Global Value Chains', *European Journal of Development Research*, 28/4: 625–645.

Kinkel, S. and Maloca, S. (2009). 'Drivers and Antecedents of Manufacturing Offshoring and Backshoring: A German Perspective', *Journal of Purchasing and Supply Management*, 15/3: 154–165.

Kohli, A. (2020). *Imperialism and the Developing World: How Britain and The United States Shaped the Global Periphery*. Oxford, New York: Oxford University Press.

Kuan, M.L. (2017). 'Manufacturing and Services in Singapore's Economy: Twin Engines of Growth and their Asymmetric Dependencies ', Ministry of Trade and Industry, Singapore.

Kuznets, S. (1966). *Modern Economic Growth: Rate, Structure and Spread*. New Haven (CT): Yale University Press.

Kvangraven, I.H. (2021). 'Beyond the Stereotype: Restating the Relevance of the Dependency Research Programme', *Development and Change*, 52/1: 76–112.

Landes, D. (1969). *The Unbound Prometheus: Technological Change and Industrial Development in Western Europe from 1750 to the Present*. Cambridge, New York: Cambridge University Press.

Lange, M. (2012). *Comparative-Historical Methods*. Thousand Oaks (CA): Sage Publishing.

Lee, K. (2019). *The Art of Economic Catch-Up: Barriers, Detours, and Leapfrogging in Innovation Systems*. Cambridge, New York: Cambridge University Press.

Lenaerts, K., Tagliapietra, S., and Wolff, G.B. (2022). 'The Global Quest for Green Growth: An Economic Policy Perspective', *Sustainability*, 14/9: 5555.

Lewis, W.A. (1954). 'Economic Development with Unlimited Supplies of Labour', *Manchester School*, 22: 139–191.

List, F. (2005 [1841]). *The National System of Political Economy*. New York: Cosimo.

Loungani, M.P., Mishra, M.S., Papageorgiou, M.C. and Wang, K. (2017). 'World Trade in Services: Evidence from a New Dataset', IMF Working Paper No. 2017/77.

Löwy, M., Akbulut, B., Fernandes, S., and Kallis, G. (2022). 'For an Ecosocialist Degrowth', *Monthly Review*, 73/11: 1 April.

MacDuffie, E. (2016). 'The Diasporic Journeys of Louise Little', *Women, Gender, and Families of Colour*, 4/2: 146–170.

Maddison, A. (2007). *Contours of the World Economy, 1-2030 AD: Essays in Macro-Economic History*. Oxford, New York: Oxford University Press.

Make UK (2022). 'Operating without Borders: Building Global Resilient Supply Chains ', Make UK, The Manufacturers' Organisation.

Mann, K. and Püttmann, L. (2018). 'Benign Effects of Automation: New Evidence from Patent Texts', available at SSRN 2959584. https://direct.mit.edu/rest/article-abstract/105/3/562/106906/Benign-Effects-of-Automation-New-Evidence-from?redirectedFrom=fulltext.

Manufacturing Metrics Expert Group (2016). 'Manufacturing Metrics Review Report', report prepared for the UK Department for Business, Innovation, and Skills.

Manyika, J., Chui, M., Miremadi, M., Bughin, J., George, K., Willmott, P., and Dewhurst, M. (2017a). *A Future That Works: AI, Automation, Employment, and Productivity*. McKinsey & Company.

Manyika, J., Lund, S., Chui, M., Bughin, J., Woetzel, P., Batra, R., Ko, R., and Sanghvi, S. (2017b). *Jobs Lost, Jobs Gained: Workforce Transitions in a Time of Automation*. McKinsey & Company.

Marconi, N., de Borja Reis, C.F., and de Araujo, E.C. (2016). 'Manufacturing and Economic Development: The Actuality of Kaldor's First and Second laws', *Structural Change and Economic Dynamics*, 37: 75–89.

Marx. K. (1990 [1867]). *Capital Volume I*. New York, London: Penguin Classics.

Mayer, J. (2009). 'Policy Space: What, for What, and Where?', *Development Policy Review*, 27/4: 373–395.

Mazzucato, M. (2013). *The Entrepreneurial State: Debunking Public vs Private Sector Myths*. London: Anthem Press.

McKinsey (2018). 'Digital Manufacturing: Escaping Pilot Purgatory', McKinsey & Company.

McMillan, M., Rodrik, D., and Sepulveda, C. (2017). 'Structural Change, Fundamentals, and Growth: A Framework and Country Studies', Policy Research Working Paper No. 8041. Washington, DC: World Bank.

Meadows, D.H., Meadows, D.L., Randers, J., and Behrens, W.W. (1972). *The Limits to Growth*. New York: Universe Books.

Meckstroth, D.J. (2017). 'The Manufacturing Value Chain Is Much Bigger Than You Think! ', Manufacturers Alliance Foundation, Arlington, VA.

Mezzadri, A. (2016). 'Class, Gender and the Sweatshop: On the Nexus between Labour Commodification and Exploitation', *Third World Quarterly*, 37/10: 1877–1900.

Milberg, W. (2008). 'Shifting Sources and Uses of Profits: Sustaining US Financialization with Global Value Chains', *Economy and Society*, 37/3: 420–451.

Milberg, W. and Winkler, D. (2013). *Outsourcing Economics: Global Value Chains in Capitalist Development*. Cambridge, New York: Cambridge University Press.

Milberg, W., Jiang, X., and Gereffi, G. (2014). 'Industrial Policy in the Era of Vertically Specialized Industrialization', in J. Salasr-Xirinachs, I. Nübler, and R. Kozul-Wright (eds), *Transforming Economies: Making Industrial Policy Work for Growth, Jobs and Development*. Geneva: UN Conference for Trade and Development, International Labour Organization, pp. 151–178.

Miller, B. and Atkinson, R.D. (2013). 'Are Robots Taking Our Jobs, or Making Them?', Information Technology and Innovation Foundation.

Miroudot, S. and Cadestin, C. (2017). 'Services in Global Value Chains: From Inputs to Value-Creating Activities', OECD Trade Policy Papers No. 198. Paris: OECD Publishing.

Morris, M. and Staritz, C. (2019). 'Industrialization Paths and Industrial Policy for Developing Countries in Global Value Chains', in S. Ponte, G. Gereffi, and G. Raj-Reichert (eds), *Handbook on Global Value Chains*. Cheltenham: Edward Elgar, pp. 506–520.

Myrdal, G. (1957). *Economic Theory and Underdeveloped Regions*. London: Duckworth.

Naudé, W. (2010). 'Industrial Policy: Old and New Issues', World Institute for Development Economics Research (WIDER) Working Paper No. 2010/106. Helsinki: United Nations University (UNU)–WIDER.

Nayak, R. and Padhye, R. (eds) (2017). *Automation in Garment Manufacturing*. Sawston: Woodhead Publishing.

Nayyar, D. (2013). *Catch Up: Developing Countries in the World Economy*. Oxford, New York: Oxford University Press.

Nayyar, G., Cruz, M., and Zhu, L. (2018). 'Does Premature Deindustrialization Matter? The Role of Manufacturing versus Services in Development', Policy Research Working Paper No. 8596. Washington, DC: World Bank.

Nayyar, G., Hallward-Driemeier, M., and Davies, E. (2021). *At Your Service? The Promise of Services-Led Development*. Washington, DC: World Bank.

Nem Singh, J. and Chen, G.C. (2018). 'State-Owned Enterprises and the Political Economy of State–State Relations in the Developing World', *Third World Quarterly*, 39/6: 1077–1097.

Newman, N., Fletcher, R., Schulz, A., Andi, S., and Nielsen, R.K. (2020). *Reuters Institute Digital News Report 2020*. Oxford: Reuters Institute, University of Oxford.

Nolan, P., Zhang, J., and Liu, C. (2008). 'The Global Business Revolution, the Cascade Effect, and the Challenge for Firms from Developing Countries', *Cambridge Journal of Economics*, 32/1: 29–47.

Noman, A., Botchwey, K., Stein, H. and Stiglitz, J. (eds) (2011). *Good Growth and Governance in Africa: Rethinking Development Strategies*. Oxford, New York: Oxford University Press.

Nurkse, R. (1961). *Problems of Capital Formation in Underdeveloped Countries*. Oxford, New York: Oxford University Press.

Nussbaum, M.C. and Sen. A. (1993). *The Quality of Life*. Oxford, New York: Oxford University Press.

Ocampo, J.A., Rada, C., and Taylor, L. (2009). *Growth and Policy in Developing Countries: A Structuralist Approach*. New York: Columbia University Press.

OECD (2002). *Foreign Direct Investment for Development: Maximising Benefits, Minimising Costs*. Paris: OECD.

OECD (2013). *Interconnected Economies: Benefitting from Global Value Chains*. Paris: OECD.

Okonwo, R.L. (1980). 'The Garvey Movement in British West-Africa', *Journal of African History*, 21/1: 105–117.

Oqubay, A. (2015). *Made in Africa: Industrial Policy in Ethiopia*. Oxford, New York: Oxford University Press.

Pagano, U. (2014). 'The Crisis of Intellectual Monopoly Capitalism', *Cambridge Journal of Economics*, 38/6: 1409–1429.

Palacios, J.J. (2001). 'Production Networks and Industrial Clustering in Developing Regions: Electronics Manufacturing in Guadalajara', Universidad de Guadalajara, México.

Park, S.-H. and Chan, K. (1989). 'A Cross-Country Input–Output Analysis of Intersectoral Relationships between Manufacturing and Services and Their Employment Implications', *World Development*, 17/2: 199–212.

Parschau, C. and Hauge, C. (2020). 'Is Automation Stealing Manufacturing Jobs? Evidence from South Africa's Apparel Industry. *Geoforum*, 115: 120–131.

Paus, E.A. and Gallagher, K.P. (2008). 'Missing Links: Foreign Investment and Industrial Development in Costa Rica and Mexico', *Studies in Comparative International Development*, 43/1: 53–80.

Peres, W. and Primi, A. (2009). 'Theory and Practice of Industrial Policy: Evidence from the Latin American Experience ', Santiago: UN Economic Commission for Latin America and the Caribbean.

Pettifor, A. (2019). *The Case for the Green New Deal*. London, New York: Verso Books.

Pilat, D. and Wolfl, A. (2005). 'Measuring the Interaction between Manufacturing and Services', OECD Science, Technology and Industry Working Papers No. 2005/05. Paris: OECD.

Pilling, D. (2019). *The Growth Delusion: The Wealth and Well-Being of Nations*. London, New York: Bloomsbury Publishing.

Piva, M. and Vivarelli, M. (2017). 'Technological Change and Employment: Were Ricardo and Marx Right?', IZA Discussion Paper No. 10471.

Pisano, G. and Shih, W. (2012). *Producing Prosperity: Why America Needs a Manufacturing Renaissance*. Cambridge (MA): Harvard Business Review Press.

Pollin, R. (2015). *Greening the Global Economy*. Cambridge (MA): MIT Press.

Pollin, R. (2020). 'An Industrial Policy Framework to Advance a Global Green New Deal', in A. Oqubay, C. Cramer, H.-J. Chang, and R. Kozul-Wright (eds), *The Oxford Handbook of Industrial Policy*. Oxford, New York: Oxford University Press, pp. 394–428.

Prebisch, R. (1950). *The Economic Development of Latin America and Its Principal Problems*. New York: United Nations.

PwC (PricewaterhouseCoopers) (2017). *UK Economic Outlook: March 2017*. London: PricewaterhouseCoopers.

Reinert, E.S. (2007). *How Rich Countries Got Rich and Why Poor Countries Stay Poor*. London: Constable.

Reinert, E. and Kvangraven, I. H. (eds.) (2023). *A Modern Guide to Uneven Economic Development*. Cheltenham: Edward Elgar.

Rekiso, Z.S. (2019). 'Economics of Late Development and Industrialization: Putting Gebrehiwot Baykedagn (1886–1919) in Context', *Cambridge Journal of Economics*, 43/1: 223–248.

Rifkin, J. (2019). *The Green New Deal: Why the Fossil Fuel Civilization Will Collapse by 2028, and the Bold Economic Plan to Save Life on Earth*. New York: St. Martin's Press.

Roberts, A. and Lamp, N. (2021). *Six Faces of Globalization: Who Wins, Who Loses, and Why It Matters*. Cambridge (MA): Harvard University Press.

Rodrik, D. (2014). 'Green Industrial Policy', *Oxford Review of Economic Policy*, 30/3: 469–491.

Rosenberg, N. (1982). *Inside the Black Box: Technology and Economics*. Cambridge, New York: Cambridge University Press.

Rowthorn, R. and Ramaswamy, R. (1999). 'Growth, Trade, and Deindustrialisation', *IMF Staff Papers*, 46/1: 18–41.

Schlogl, L. and Sumner, A. (2020). *Disrupted Development and the Future of Inequality in the Age of Automation*. London: Palgrave Macmillan.

Schmelzer, M., Vetter, A., and Vansintjan, A. (2022). *The Future is Degrowth: A Guide to a World beyond Capitalism*. London, New York: Verso Books.

Schumpeter, J.A. (1983 [1934]). *The Theory of Economic Development*. Piscataway (NJO: Transaction Publishers.

Schumpeter, J.A. (2010 [1942]). *Capitalism, Socialism and Democracy*. Eastford (CT): Martino Fine Books.

Schwab, K. (2016). *The Fourth Industrial Revolution*. Cologny: World Economic Forum.

Selwyn. B. (2017). *The Struggle for Development*. Cambridge (MA): Polity Press.

Selwyn, B. (2019). 'Poverty Chains and Global Capitalism', *Competition & Change*, 23/1: 71–97.

Selwyn, B. and Leyden, D. (2022). 'Oligopoly-Driven Development: The World Bank's *Trading for Development in the Age of Global Value Chains* in Perspective', *Competition & Change*, 26/2: 174–196.

Shadlen, K.C. (2005). 'Exchanging Development for Market Access? Deep Integration and Industrial Policy under Multilateral and Regional-Bilateral Trade Agreements', *Review of International Political Economy*, 12/5: 750–775.

Short, R. (1983). 'The Role of Public Enterprises: An International Statistical Comparison', Department Memorandum Series 8384. Washington, DC: International Monetary Fund.

Slaughter, M.J. (2010). 'How US Multinational Companies Strengthen the US Economy', Business Roundtable and the United States Council for International Business.

Smith. A. (1982 [1776]). *The Wealth of Nations: Books I–III*. New York, London: Penguin Classics.

Solberg, C. (1979). *Oil and Nationalism in Argentina*. Stanford (CA): Stanford University Press.

Starrs, S. (2014). 'The Chimera of Global Convergence', *New Left Review*, 87/1: 81–96.

Steinmann, Z.J., Schipper, A.M., Hauck, M., Giljum, S., Wernet, G., and Huijbregts, M.A. (2017). 'Resource Footprints Are Good Proxies of Environmental Damage', *Environmental Science & Technology*, 51/11: 6360–6366.

Stiglitz, J.E. and Lin, J.Y. (eds) (2013). *The Industrial Policy Revolution I: The Role of Government Beyond Ideology*. Basingstoke: Palgrave Macmillan.

Susskind, R.R. and Susskind, D. (2015). *The Future of the Professions: How Technology Will Transform the Work of Human Experts*. Oxford, New York: Oxford University Press.

Suwandi, I. (2019). *Value Chains: The New Economic Imperialism*. New York: Monthly Review Press.

Szirmai, A. (2012). 'Industrialisation as an Engine of Growth in Developing Countries, 1950–2005', *Structural Change and Economic Dynamics*, 23/4: 406–420.

Szirmai, A. and Verspagen, B. (2015). 'Manufacturing and Economic Growth in Developing Countries, 1950–2005', *Structural Change and Economic Dynamics*, 34: 46–59.

Szreter, S. and Mooney, G. (1998). 'Urbanization, Mortality, and the Standard of Living Debate: New Estimates of the Expectation of Life at Birth in Nineteenth-Century British Cities', *Economic History Review*, 51/1: 84–112.

Taglioni, D. and Winkler, D. (2016). *Making Global Value Chains Work for Development*. Washington, DC: World Bank.

Tate, W.L. (2014). 'Offshoring and Reshoring: US Insights and Research Challenges', *Journal of Purchasing and Supply Management*, 20/1: 66–68

Teece, D. (2010). 'Technological Innovation and the Theory of the Firm: The Role of Enterprise-Level Knowledge, Complementarities, and (Dynamic) Capabilities', in N. Rosenberg and B. Hall (eds), *Handbook of the Economics of Innovation*. Amsterdam: North–Holland, pp. 679–730.

Tregenna, F. (2009). 'Characterising Deindustrialisation: An Analysis of Change in Manufacturing Employment and Output Internationally', *Cambridge Journal of Economics*, 33/3: 433–466.

UNCTAD (United Nations Conference on Trade and Development) (2017). *Trade and Development Report 2017: Beyond Austerity: Towards a Global New Deal*. Geneva: United Nations Conference on Trade and Development.

UNCTAD (2019). *World Investment Report 2019: Special Economic Zones*. Geneva: United Nations Conference on Trade and Development.

UNCTAD (2020). *The Impact of COVID-19 on Trade and Development: Transitioning to a New Normal*. Geneva: United Nations Conference on Trade and Development.

UNECA (United Nations Economic Commission for Africa) (2015). *Economic Report on Africa 2015: Industrializing through Trade*. Addis Ababa: United Nations Economic Commission for Africa.

UNIDO (United Nations Industrial Development Organization) (2020). *Industrial Development Report 2020: Industrializing in the Digital Age*. Vienna: United Nations Industrial Development Organization.

UNIDO (2022). *Industrial Development Report 2022: The Future of Industrialization in a Post-Pandemic World*. Vienna: United Nations Industrial Development Organization.

United States Census Bureau (2022). https://www.census.gov/newsroom/stories/poverty-awareness-month.html

Wade, R.H. (1990). *Governing the Market: Economic Theory and the Role of Government in East Asian Industrialization*. Princeton (NJ), Oxford: Princeton University Press.

Wade, R.H. (2003). 'What Strategies Are Viable for Developing Countries Today? The World Trade Organization and the Shrinking of "Development Space"', *Review of International Political Economy*, 10/4: 621–644.

Wade, R.H. (2019). 'Catch-Up and Constraints in the Twentieth and Twenty-First Centuries', in A. Oqubay and K. Ohno (eds), *How Nations Learn: Technological*

Learning, Industrial Policy, and Catch-Up. Oxford, New York: Oxford University Press, pp. 15–37.

Wallerstein, I. (1974). 'The Rise and Future Demise of the World Capitalist System: Concepts for Comparative Analysis', *Comparative Studies in Society and History*, 16/4: 387–415.

Weber, I., Semieniuk, G., Westland, T., and Liang, J. (2021). 'Why Your Exporter Matters: Persistence in Productive Capabilities across Two Eras of Globalization', Working Paper No. 2021–02. University of Massachusetts, Department of Economics, Amherst, MA.

Weiss, M. and Cattaneo, C. (2017). 'Degrowth: Taking Stock and Reviewing an Emerging Academic Paradigm', *Ecological Economics*, 137: 220–230.

Whitefoot, K., Valdivia, W., and Adam, G. (2015). 'Innovation and Manufacturing Labour: A Value Chain Perspective', Washington, DC: Brookings Institution.

Wiedmann, T. and Lenzen, M. (2018). 'Environmental and Social Footprints of International Trade', *Nature Geoscience*, 11/5: 314–321.

Willcocks, L. (2020). 'Robo-Apocalypse Cancelled? Reframing the Automation and Future of Work Debate', *Journal of Information Technology*, 35/4: 286–302.

Wilson, P.A. (1992). *Exports and Local Development: Mexico's New Maquiladoras*. Austin (TX): University of Texas Press.

World Bank (1993). *The East Asian Miracle: Economic Growth and Public Policy*. Washington, DC: World Bank.

World Bank (2008). *The Growth Report: Strategies for Sustained Growth and Inclusive Development*. Washington, DC: World Bank.

World Bank (2012). *Inclusive Green Growth: The Pathway to Sustainable Development*. Washington, DC: World Bank.

World Bank (2016). *World Development Report 2016: Digital Dividends*. Washington, DC: World Bank.

World Bank (2020). *Trading for Development in the Age of Global Value Chains*. Washington, DC: World Bank.

World Economic Forum (2020). *The Future of Jobs Report 2020*. Cologny: World Economic Forum.

WTO (World Trade Organization) (2013). *World Trade Report 2013: Factors Shaping the Future of World Trade*. Geneva: World Trade Organization.

WTO (2019). *World Trade Report 2019: The Future of Services Trade*. Geneva: World Trade Organization.

WWF (World Wildlife Fund) (2018). *Living Planet Report 2018: Aiming Higher*. Gland, Switzerland: World Wildlife Fund.

WWF (2021). 'In Too Deep: What We Know, and Don't Know, About Deep Seabed Mining', WWF International.

Zewde, B. *Pioneers of Change in Ethiopia: The Reformist Intellectuals of the Early Twentieth Century*. Ohio: Ohio University Press.

Zuboff, S. (2019). *The Age of Surveillance Capitalism: The Fight for a Human Future at the Frontier of Power*. London, New York: Profile Books.

Index

For the benefit of digital users, indexed terms that span two pages (e.g., 52–53) may, on occasion, appear on only one of those pages.